LIFE'S
KALEIDOSCOPE

T0380396

LIFE'S
KALEIDOSCOPE

AN ANTHOLOGY BY WRITERS IN GOOD COMPANY

JoLynne Buehring; Loretta M. Ogao; Tatiana
Koslova; Lana Ray; Mary Alexander

To order additional copies of this book, contact:
Xlibris Corporation
1-888-795-4274
www.Xlibris.com
Orders@Xlibris.com
36029

CONTENTS

PEOPLE

PLACES

THINGS

AND MORE

INTRODUCTION

Life is vibrant and full. We are all different and yet we are the same. Our group met as strangers, but we have become friends and have a common interest in writing. Coming from different walks of life and having the desire to capture and share with family, friends and others glimpses of our life's encounters, ideas, thoughts, and feelings, we have compiled this anthology of creative non-fiction.

Each story and poem is different, yet many of us have experienced or have been affected by something similar. We all gain from these exposures whether we are aware of it or not. We find pleasure in reading about others and things, often applying what we have acquired to improve not only our lives, but the lives of those around us. May this be a gift to all who read it and perhaps encourage others to write their stories, enriching the lives of others and future generations.

ACKNOWLEDGEMENTS

We would like to express our gratitude to those who have helped us directly or indirectly, individually and as a group, toward our goals, including the following: Terri Mueller, Kathy Baccaro, Kathy Swackhammer, and Wesseleen Stookesberry, and in memorium, our friend, Tatiana Koslova, who is no longer with us.

PEOPLE

PEOPLE

IN MEMORY OF YEE WEE

The incessant wind blew pieces of tumbleweed and trash across the barren, neglected cemetery. The Arizona sun, hot even on Memorial Day, beat down on my straight, black hair. Few of the graves showed any sign of care, and those that did were the big plots of the prominent Hispanic families who had settled in the area. Generations of headstones were covered with bright plastic flowers behind ornate wrought iron fences. They were a poignant contrast to the desert weed-covered grave in front of me. The simplicity of the concrete headstone almost seemed dismissive. Except for the extra line . . .

YEE WEE
Born in China
Died February 20, 1968
SEE YOU TOMORROW

*　　*　　*

Gleeson, Arizona, once called Turquoise, was the booming center of the southeastern Arizona mining industry in the late 1800s and was already long past its peak before World War II. While it was thriving, the area attracted immigrants desperate for the golden opportunities they had been led to believe they would find. Few were left; leaving the area to those whose blood sprang from the hot, dry soil, and the handful of ranching families who were there before the mines.

Research for my work at the University of Arizona put me on the trail of Chinese immigrants who found their way to Arizona. Residents in the small surrounding communities directed me to the oldest of the early ranchers, known by everyone as Old Earl, and his brother, Dan.

I found them on the front porch of the small frame house that guarded the gate onto the ranch. All showed signs of age. The house had weathered to nearly the color of the desert around it. The heavy gate showed rust through the many coats of chipped paint. Earl and Dan were also a weathered tan, in work-bleached Levis, faded plaid, western shirts and cowboy boots so broken-in they had wear holes in the toes. Their ages seemed immaterial after one look at bright blue eyes, which missed nothing and showed interest in everything.

Once we got the "How Dos" as Earl called them, out of the way, we settled into our creaking rocking chairs for a "good chin-wag", obviously Earl's favorite activity. Dan seemed shyer and a little more reticent, leaving Earl in the role of spokesman with his country boy drawl.

"We only got Yee Wee's story in bits and pieces. The Chinese Exclusion Act of 1882 banned Chinese immigration. He told us he came from Canton, China after that and was smuggled onto the docks in San Francisco Bay in a whiskey barrel. We're not sure just when."

Yee Wee eventually made his way to what the locals called the Chinese Gardens near Fairbanks, Arizona where a railroad spur was being built. Always outcasts and unwelcome in the neighboring communities, the Chinese were resourceful for survival and planted extensive gardens, hauling the needed water from the nearby San Pedro River.

Trouble of some sort encouraged Yee Wee to move on, finally settling in Gleeson. The miners welcomed his "eating house" where he cooked simple meals.

"There was a sign on the side of Yee Wee's building that said, 'YOU KILL IT, WEE COOK IT.' And he did, it didn't matter if it was snake, javelina, bear, rabbit, deer or some other of critter. Any vegetables he fixed came from his gardens. He watered them twice a day, carried water from the community well in a five gallon can on a stick over his shoulder."

Dan spoke up in a quiet voice. "We rode on the wagon with him to Tombstone when he went for supplies. Dad drove the team, and Earl and I rode in back in the wagon bed."

Earl took the cue and picked up that part of the story. "Supplies came in on the rail spur and once in a while, there would be mail from China for Yee Wee, along with bundles of Chinese newspapers, you know, with that funny writing, wrapped in a strange kind of rough brown paper.

"Yee Wee didn't let people know much about himself and didn't talk much, but he seemed to like us boys. He tolerated us hanging around whenever we could get away from ranch chores. He usually treated us to some penny candy when we went to Tombstone."

"Another Chinaman showed up one day," Dan put in, obviously envisioning a scene for the long ago. "He and Yee Wee got into an argument under that big oak out back of his building. When the dust settled, the stranger was dead." Shaking his head, he continued, "Nothing was done about it, no investigation or anything. The attitude then was why worry about another dead Chinaman. The Chinese were being persecuted all over the West, so the stranger was one less to be bothered with."

"We found out later, those newspaper wrappings Yee Wee got from China were some form of opium, and we figured that had something to do with the fight," Earl put in.

As the mines played out, Gleeson was gradually abandoned, the tent town was folded up, and many of the adobe buildings began a slow settle back into the desert floor. One by one, families moved away and businesses closed. Finally, Yee Wee had too few customers to keep his doors open, and he said he was too old to start over.

Back in 1901, Arizona law forbade intermarriage between Chinese and Anglos. Brides could be brought from China, but Yee Wee seemed to feel a need to keep a very low visibility to authorities. He continued his solitary life.

"By that time we could tell Yee Wee was sick," said Earl, going on with the story. "He just seemed to get thinner and thinner, probably TB or something. Maybe he was just wearing out. Dan and I took turns seeing that he had firewood and water. Whenever we went into town, we'd stop to see if he wanted us to pick up anything for him. He always paid for his groceries, but he was tight with a nickel and he didn't miss checking the ticket to see how much we paid for things. He always complained about the cost of something, or told us he got a better price at a different store.

"He didn't trust banks, once said he liked to be able to move on if he needed to, so he put his money into bearer bonds he kept with his cash in a metal box. It was the size of a cigar box and he kept it under his mattress."

Dan spoke up again, "Every time we got ready to leave after we'd stopped by, Yee Wee always said, 'I see you tomorrow.' The last time I saw him, I told him I'd be gone for two or three days to take care of business in Tucson.

"He got really mad and almost yelled, 'NO, I see you tomorrow!'"

"When we got back from Tucson, Yee Wee was dead and his little house had been emptied by the Sheriff. We never did know what became of his belongings, including his metal box. We did find out his real name was Wong Him, but he'll always be Yee Wee to us. By our best guess, he was about 106 years old when he died."

I made my way, once again, through the weeds of the desolate cemetery, pulling dry tumbleweeds away from the plain concrete marker. In the Chinese custom, I dropped a few coins on the grave to join the other weathered pennies, dimes and quarters.

"You just wait, Yee Wee. I'll tell your story, and about all the other Chinese in Arizona, the ones who were shut in a railroad car on a siding and left in the hot sun, and the ones who were hung or shot just because they were Chinese. Soon there will be a book about you, written by me, Jenny Wong."

Palms together, I kowtowed as Grandmother taught me.

"*Uncle*, I see you tomorrow!"

                                                            JoLynne

CHARLEY LONG NOSE

Charley Long Nose squatted near the ashes of the shelter and stared at his gnarled hands He didn't have the white man's word for the condition. He only knew they hurt on this cold morning and were a sure sign of his seventy summers of life.

The tribe burned everything yesterday before the farewell feast to honor his elder brother, Walks Far. Walks Far had four summers more than Charley. In their youth he taught Charley all he knew about living with the land. Their parents died when Charley still had a girl's voice, he guessed he had no more than ten summers then. But Walks Far caught the white man's coughing sickness. It finally took his life.

Their Cocopah brethren left early this morning to move south, hoping that the River Mother would have replenished the earth at its delta. Charley stayed behind. It was time. His painful stride would only slow them down on the long trek.

He gave out a long sigh as he reached down and lifted the worn leather pouch that held what remained of his worldly goods; a knife, a seashell amulet, some wooden matches from the trader's store upriver, two dried fish, and some dried wild berries. He broke off a piece of fish and chewed it slowly. He poked a stick into the ashes as he rocked back and forth in his squatting position.

It had been done well—the burning—according to the long tradition of his people. They kept no permanent residence. When their spirit left their body all that bound them to this earth was committed to the flames. Even his staying behind was keeping tradition. He was old. He no longer could help his people and it was not honorable to be a burden.

He swallowed a bit of the fish he'd been chewing and raised his canvas water pouch to his lips. The water must last him until he made the long walk to the river. In an earlier time he would not have thought it long.

Now he will do well if he reaches it by midday. The white man's city that they gave the Indian name Yuma was just a small distance upriver. He had been there briefly many seasons before. He wondered if it was still crowded with people coming and going in all directions. *I don't think I am ready to die*, he thought, *and there is no one here to send my spirit in the flames. Perhaps, before it is my time, I should see what the white men are doing in their city and if my old friend from across the big water is still living.*

The sun was high overhead when he dipped his water bag into an eddy at the bank of the river. The white man did some things right. This canvas bag and sulfur matches were improvements over hide pouches and fire flints. He pulled his handmade leather boots off and put his feet in the water. What a change from the chill of the morning to the heat of the day. The current in the eddy was refreshing to his tired and sore feet. He ate a few bites of his dried fish before pulling on his boots and heading toward Yuma.

He reached the city sooner than he anticipated. It seemed like the city had moved out to meet him. He didn't remember it spreading out so far. On the main street noisy automobiles made crossing hazardous. There appeared to be more shade on the far side but when he started to cross a blaring horn honked at him and the driver hollered "Go back to the Res, Chief! I nearly ran you down!"

This was not as he recalled from his earlier time here—more people, more noise. The women dressed strangely in short dresses that exposed their white legs. Their hair was cut short and some had yellow hair with lots of tight curls. Charley just shook his head in bewilderment. When he was here so long ago there had been as many horse and wagons as automobiles. Now no horses or wagons, just noisy automobiles. He looked for the Chinee man's eating place that he remembered. The Chinee had befriended him back then and gave him a large bowl of rice. Now his thoughts took him back to that time:

I approached the eating place while looking at the many strange sights of this white man's world. Suddenly a splash of water hit me from a doorway and a funny little man stepped out and exclaimed, "Oh, so solly! I not see you. Please to forgive. Come, come. I dry you."

The little man beckoned me inside and pulled a chair for me from one of many tables. He said, "I am Yong Soo. What is your name?"

I understood enough of the white man's language to tell him in Cocopah, "I am Long Nose."

That made no sense to him. I pointed to my nose and drew my finger down it as I repeated "Long Nose."

He flashed a broad smile and said it in white man's words "Long Nose. But you are good man. I call you Charley . . . Charley Long Nose."

He grabbed a large cloth from a table and offered it to me to dry myself. He had been throwing out water from washing the floors when I stepped in the way of his door. Again he said, "I so solly. You hungry? I make you rice bowl." He made hand moves like eating, so I smiled at him and nodded my head. And now I had a white man's name.

. . . .

Charley wasn't sure if he would recognize the eating place but walking along the street he became aware of curious and familiar smells, like the Chinee man's place. It didn't look the same. The doorway was bigger and painted bright red. A broad colorful sign was fixed above the door. He took a chance and pushed the door open. A voice said, "We are open. Come right in."

A moment passed as Charley's eyes adjusted to the dim interior. The tables were set with white cloth covers. The voice he heard came from a young man wearing clothes of shiny bright colored material like Charley remembered his former friend wore, only this man looked to have maybe fifty summers and most of his front was covered by a large white wrap that tied in back. He was too young to be Yong Soo.

The young man said, "Please have a seat," and gestured to a chair. "How may I help you?"

Charley stood by the door and said, "I am looking for Yong Soo."

"Oh, you want my father. He is not here but I can get him for you. What is your name? Please sit. I will call him." Charley spoke his name and again was motioned toward the chair, the man waiting until Charley sat down.

The young man disappeared in the back of the place and Charley heard him call, "Father, an old Indian is here asking for you. He says his name is Charley Long Nose. Will you see him?"

The reply was muffled, but when the man came back he was smiling. "My father will be here in a few minutes. He said to ask if you would like a bowl of rice?"

Charley was not inclined to refuse. In minutes a steaming bowl of rice with chicken and vegetables was set before him. Charley nodded his thanks and quickly attacked the savory dish with the porcelain spoon set by the bowl.

He lifted the bowl to his lips and was draining the last broth when Yong Soo came into the room from the back. He was bent nearly double with the infirmities of age but he raised his head as he approached Charley and beamed a bright smile.

"I remember you, my friend." With that greeting he ran a finger along his nose and then pointed it toward Charley. "It has been long time since we met."

Charley had learned much of the white man's speech over the years, but Yong Soo's curious accent was hard to follow. His smile and hospitality were not hard to follow.

Yong Soo sat with him and the two old men found common ground. Each was separated from their birth culture and forced to find their way in this white man's world. Yong Soo came from China as a youth to build the railroads. When the railway came to Yuma he had an injury and was left behind. As the only Chinese in the area he was very lonely and hungry. He first earned his food by doing laundry for the many single men in the territory. Later he saved enough the start his eating place and to send for a wife from China. His son now ran the restaurant and had been doing so since Yong Soo's wife died.

Charley explained about his people moving on without him.

"Then you have no place to live?" Yong Soo exclaimed.

Charley shrugged.

"You must stay with me," he declared.

As quickly as that it was settled. Charley felt surprised, humbled, and yet a bit embarrassed, "I have nothing to share for your kindness."

"That's okay," insisted Yong Soo, "Plesident Loosevelt will give you money for what you need."

Charley shook his head. "I don't understand. Who is this who gives money?"

Yong Soo beckoned to his son, "Yong Lin, come tell Charley about Plesident give money."

Yong Lin pulled a chair from an adjacent table and sat with them. His look held both respect and amusement. "My father is trying to tell you about the new program that President Roosevelt has instituted called 'Social Security.' There are too many people without jobs right now and many old people hungry. Among programs he has started to give people work, he was able to get Congress to enact this new plan to help those in need now and in the future. Every worker pays something into the plan and when they are old, as my father is, the money comes back to them doubled by the government."

"But I have not paid to this plan," Charley protested.

"That is why he added to the plan for persons like yourself to have a little income from Supplemental Security. If you have a permanent place to live you can sign up for the benefit."

"I do not know how to do that," Charley replied.

"If you decide to stay here with us," Yong Lin offered, "I can go with you to the office and help you get signed up. My father has done everything for me and if he calls you his friend then I too am your friend."

That is how Charley Long Nose came to be the first Cocopah to live permanently in one place and the first to collect Social Security benefits from the government.

When his people heard of this many decided to move to towns and keep their old people with them, no longer leaving them behind in the desert.

Mary

OUR SPECIAL CHILD

Sam and Martha were childless. They had been married nearly thirteen years. Martha lost a baby about five years ago when she was almost three month pregnant They felt a great loss after trying so hard. After her third miscarriage, Martha was told that she had a twisted uterus and her diabetes was not under good control. She also had a medical history of asthma and frequent urinary tract infections. Sam had a problem of a low sperm count. Their doctor told them that under these circumstances, the likelihood of them having their own baby would be almost impossible. Sam and Martha were sad and discouraged but did not feel hopeless. After all, miracles can happen.

Being in the military and not close to family, they helped their friends with children by babysitting. Martha loved watching and playing with them, especially the babies. After several months, like many couples desiring a child, they decided to go to the infertility clinic.

In the summer of 1993, Martha felt terrible and went to see her doctor. Martha had been a patient of Dr. Smith for a number of years now. After running some tests and examining Martha, Dr. Smith spoke to her in his office.

"Do you really want a baby?" he asked."

"Of course," Martha replied. "but I haven't been feeling well and wonder if my diabetes is worse or I'm developing another health problem," she said. "Am I?" she asked.

"Well, your diabetes is not too unusual for you, but you do have another issue to think about," he said as he smiled. "You do have a slight urine infection which needs to be treated. But, among the tests done, one was a pregnancy test, and the result is positive. You are pregnant Martha," he said smilingly.

Martha could hardly believe what she heard. Was this for real, she thought? Dr. Smith proceeded to tell her about carefully monitoring her during this pregnancy and what she needed to do about taking care of herself because of her history.

"Are you sure?, she asked excitedly.

"You are pregnant, Martha," he repeated. "You know you're going to have to be very careful about what you eat and the physical things you do. Here are some instructions for you to follow until your next visit." Martha slowly reached out for the instructions still with an expression of disbelief.

"Don't forget to read them with your husband. It's important that you follow them and that Sam understands them too."

"Oh, thank you, thank you so much, Dr. Smith. You've made my day!" Martha left the doctor's office ecstatic, eager to share the news with her husband.

Martha arrived home shortly before Sam. He was elated after Martha told him the wonderful news. Though overjoyed, they promised each other they would not make any preparations for the baby yet. Martha's health was more important at this time. Both were fearful that something might happen again if they did not heed what the doctor said.

That evening, they read and discussed the instructions Dr. Smith gave Martha until they understood what they needed to do. They also felt staying calm and being prayerful were also important.

This pregnancy was not quite like her previous pregnancies. Yes, she did experience some nausea and vomiting, but Martha felt different from the last time and couldn't quite explain it. She had more mood swings and felt more exhausted all the time. Sam took her symptoms in stride and tried harder to be patient, helpful, and tolerant. It was not easy.

One day when Martha went to register for the prenatal classes, Sam had an idea. He cleaned out the extra room, rearranged the few pieces of furniture there was, and decorated it with a beautiful bouquet of artificial flowers and some family photos. He even found a picture of a crib from a magazine, framed it, then placed it on the wall.

When Martha came home, Sam had the door to the room slightly opened and was sitting reading the paper. Martha, tired, hungry, and irritable, was annoyed seeing him doing nothing and just said "Hi!"

Sam stood up quickly, greeted her with a big hug, and then asked her to close her eyes.

"What for?" she asked grumpily. "What are you up to?"

"Please, just do it and I'll tell you in a minute," he said. Reluctantly, she did. He then led her to the extra room. Once there, "Open your eyes now," he instructed. Martha opened her eyes.

"Ooh, this is so beautiful! What a pleasant surprise! Thank you so much," she said. She felt badly for being annoyed with him earlier but glad she had not said anything to him. She turned, and they embraced. Happily, they stood silently looking around the room.

Martha required more bedrest, closer monitoring of her diabetes and diet, no lifting anything over five pounds, and less physical activities. She did quite well and felt ok.

She even started "talking" to her baby expressing her love, and things she looked forward to as a family. She sang songs like "Rock-a-bye, Baby," and "I Love You Truly," while rubbing her abdomen. A very special relationship and bonding began.

Her visits to the doctor were routine. She had an ultrasound when she was approximately 28 weeks pregnant. It showed a single pregnancy with no obvious abnormalities noted. Baby's sex was identified. They named him "Jeffrey." Martha continued to be diligent in following her instructions. Sam was very supportive even if he had more chores to do when he came home from work and was tired.

Approximately two weeks later, Martha started experiencing some periodic, inconsistent cramping and felt that something was not right. "I'm taking you to the doctor," Sam said, "we're not going to take any chances." Sam called her doctor before leaving home. Dr. Smith instructed him to take her to the emergency room and he will meet them there. Sam then went to help Martha get up from the couch and assisted her walking to the garage and into the car.

Upon arrival at the emergency room, they had a wheel chair waiting for her. Martha was immediately taken into a room and prepared for an examination. Dr. Smith came in shortly after. She had a mild contraction and was most uncomfortable during the examination. She was admitted to the hospital. It was a very trying time.

In spite of everything that was done, Martha went into early labor. Sam was not able to be there when the baby was born. The baby was vaginally delivered without complications. However, the newborn had no cry, no significant respiratory effort and very little muscle tone. His heart rate was a little slow, and his apgar score was 2/4, or in other words, his effort to breathe, heart rate, skin color, muscle tone, and movement reactions were poor at one minute and at five minutes after birth."[1]

Dr. Blaine, the pediatrician did not know whether he would survive, but immediately took action to help the infant. He placed a tubing to provide oxygen. Baby was put in an incubator and was taken "stat" to the Newborn Intensive Care Unit where Dr. Blaine and staff went to work on him. Jeffrey survived, but not without difficulties.

Martha recovered from the delivery without any significant complications. She and Sam were able to see the baby for short periods of time only. Martha was discharged from the hospital a week later after being stabilized and felt better.

Jeffrey remained in the NICU for nearly five months. Jeffrey had weighed 4# 5 oz. a few hours after birth and was 18" tall. During his stay, numerous problems were identified. His diagnosis was determined to be "congenital myopathy" a muscle disease, usually degenerative, with "severe respiratory insufficiency and profound muscle weakness."[2] He was not expected to live. He was unable to breathe on his own requiring support by artificial ventilation. Jeffrey had a tracheotomy to help him receive enough oxygen and a gastric tube was placed through which he was fed. Jeffrey was also diagnosed as having "encephalomyopathy with an enzyme defect."[3] causing the brain and muscle functions to be abnormal also.

When he was four months old, he weighed 5# 8 oz. Jeffrey's life expectancy was determined to be twelve to twenty-four months. Knowing that, his parents wanted him home with them if it was at all possible. After much contemplation among the medical staff and the family, it was determined that this was possible.

With careful planning, preparation, and coordination with the various services, his discharge became a reality. The family had to move to housing closer to the hospital. The baby's room was modified for routine daily care and in the event of an emergency. The staffing for the various services involved was made aware of Jeffrey's condition and care. His parents were taught about his needs and trained to meet these needs. Nurses were assigned to be with the baby around the clock for a month gradually decreasing their stay to 12 hours a day for another month. Then decreasing nursing presence required only at night 10 p.m. to 7 a.m. for one month. After that, an on-call home care nurse was available day and night. The emergency room physician was accessible to the family when necessary. A respiratory technician would come to check the patient and equipment regularly on a weekly basis and as needed.

The day of his discharge was a day of celebration for Sam and Martha. He was transported from the hospital by ambulance without any problems.

Jeffrey adjusted to his new home environment without any significant problems.

"Are you scared about Jeffrey coming home?" Sam asked Martha.

"Yes and no," she said, "I just hope and pray I can do what I'm supposed to do, when I'm supposed to do it, and not be too nervous," she added. He put his arms around her shoulders and reassuringly said with a smile, "I know you can do it. I'll help you. Together we can do it."

With a wonderful support from the medical staff, friends, and family, they were able to care for him without any serious problems. Both Martha's and Sam's parents came to visit and help them occasionally. They were overjoyed to see their grandson and were very encouraging and supportive.

Gradually, Jeffrey made progress and was weaned from the ventilator for short periods at a time starting with 5 minutes three times daily, increasing the time by ten minutes every other week. His maximum time off the ventilator was 30 minutes at a time, three times a day. His breath sounds improved and he did not have to exert himself much to breathe. This was significant.

At nearly ten months old, Jeffrey had good breath sounds on the ventilator. He could also turn his head but continued to display general muscle weakness with moderate contraction in his knees. Martha immersed herself in his care. She and Sam enjoyed their baby, grateful for the little progresses he made. They loved him so much and were elated when they saw his little smile.

He showed improvement in his motor skills and was now able to move his fingers slowly and open his hands. They were even able to carry him periodically for short periods of time. These moments were extra special for all of them.

Jeffrey grew a little taller and gained some weight. Therapy and medical care continued diligently. Progress was slow and challenging, but gradual. By the time he was nineteen months old, he learned to stand with assistance for one to two minutes twice a day with braces on his lower extremities. He could sit in his wheelchair with adjustable attachments and supportive pillows properly positioned. He wore a neck brace to be comfortable. In spite of his physical deformities and condition, he was able to sit for up to fifteen minutes at a time, three or four times a day with constant observation and assistance.

Jeffrey continued to make slow but sure progress with few drawbacks and minimum problems. All adjusted quite well to the situation and the routines. The next several months were uneventful and Jeffrey's condition was relatively stable.

Two years after Jeffrey was born, his birthday was celebrated with some friends, medical staff, and family. It was a beautiful Saturday afternoon. He enjoyed watching the colorful balloons that decorated the room and seeing so many people in the room. Jeffrey sat up in his chair long enough to "blow out" the candles on his cake with the help of his Mom after everyone sang "Happy Birthday." His gifts were opened by his mom and placed in his hands. Jeffrey was delighted and "held" them for a few minutes. Although Jeffrey was unable to talk, he made a few sounds and slowly waved his hands showing his excitement. He even got a taste of his ice cream when his Mom smeared a tiny bit on his tongue. From his expressions and behavior his joyfulness was communicated. The party was tiring for him, but what a wonderful celebration for all . . . especially for him and his parents.

The next day, Jeffrey appeared more tired than usual but was able to smile after his mother gave him his feeding. Martha turned on the tape recorder to play some music. He especially liked listening to the nursery songs like "Mary Had a Little Lamb," "Jack and Jill," and others. It wasn't long before Jeffrey was asleep. The day was uneventful, but Jeffrey took longer naps than usual.

That night, Carole came on duty after being informed that Jeffrey was himself except he was more tired than usual and hardly smiled that day. The nurse checked his vital signs as usual and found everything was within normal range for him except his temperature was 99 degrees, slightly higher than the previous days. She informed Dr. Blaine who was on call.

"Carole, I think you'd better take his vital signs every 2 hours and observe his behavior. Let me know if there are any changes and continue with his usual care." This was at 8 o'clock in the evening.

"Thanks, Dr. Blaine," said Carole after she repeated his orders, "I will do that."

A sudden change in his temperature occurred at 2 o'clock a.m. It was 100.1 degrees and his pulse had increased from 86 to 110 beats per minute, respirations were now 12 breaths per minute-a decrease from 20 previously, and he was restless. Carole called Dr. Blaine and informed him of her findings. He ordered an ambulance to bring the patient to the emergency room.

Carole immediately knocked on Martha's door. "Martha, wake up, Jeffrey's temperature is up." Martha woke up, jumped out of bed and opened her door.

"His temperature is 100.1 and Dr. Blaine is sending an ambulance to take him to the hospital now," informed Carole. She then prepared Jeffrey to be transported. Martha hurriedly got dressed. By then, Sam had gotten up and dressed as Martha told him about Jeffrey's condition. Concerned and frightened, they said a quick in prayer to calm down and not think about what could happen.

Within a short time, the ambulance arrived. Jeffrey was taken to the hospital, with his parents following behind. Dr. Blaine was already in the emergency room when they arrived. His temperature was rechecked. It was up to 101.8 degrees. Beaded perspiration was evident on his forehead.

As he was being examined and treated, Martha and Sam waited anxiously in the waiting room. It seemed like hours before the doctor came to talk to them.

"Jeffrey is in very poor condition," he said. "He's being admitted. Hopefully, he'll respond favorably, but I don't know. You can come in and see him now," he added as he started to walk back into the room.

Jeffrey was admitted to the pediatric intensive care unit. He was in that unit for nearly three days. He showed no improvement. Sam and Martha spent most of their time at the hospital, seeing their son whenever they were permitted. In spite of all that was done to help him, nothing seemed to improve his condition but instead, his frail body gradually declined and his temperature increased.

Shortly after ten o'clock in the morning of the third day, Martha felt a sudden twitch in her chest then a comforting feeling overcame her while in the waiting room. She looked at her husband. He too felt something and gazed in her eyes. They held each other. Tears started to flow, knowing that their son was no longer with them physically.

When Dr. Blaine appeared, he sensed that they knew and he nodded his head. "I'm so sorry, but he's no longer with us," he said.

They hugged.

After seeing Jeffrey's lifeless body, and and spending some time with him, Sam and Martha left the hospital and slowly walked hand in hand, to their car.

In spite of their loss, Martha and Sam rejoiced in the knowledge that his love and memories will be with them forever. Their hearts were comforted and they looked forward to the future.

"How about checking out the adoption agency?" asked Sam a few weeks later.

Martha's eyes sparkled in hopeful response. "That's a great idea! Yes, let's," she said smilingly.

Loretta

---

[1]   The American Medical Assoc. Home Medical Encyclopedia, Vol. I Charles B. Clayman, MD, Random House, N. Y. 1989, pg. 31.

[2]   As above, pg. 401.

[3]   As above, pg. 410.

WHAT AM I?

Every now and then
I ask myself, what am I?
A tiny drop in a sea of life,
Or movement in the leaves
When the wind goes wild?

What am I?
A grain of sand,
Embracing oceans and the sea,
Or may be, just a shade
Under the apple tree?

Perhaps I am a murmur of a brook
That runs so clear
Among the tallest trees
Down in the dark old wood,
Or just a sound of bird
I never heard before?

But the tallest trees
Whispered softly
In my ears:
"You are all that and more
Since you're a part
Of this great world . . ."

Lana

A GRIZZLY BY ANY OTHER NAME

You've probably heard or read lots of stories about courage, but just what is it? It has several names: bravery, valor, pluck, spunk, backbone, guts, grit. We could probably come up with several more words, but they still don't tell us exactly what courage is

COURAGE is:
1) inner strength to withstand hardship
2) presence of mind in the face of great odds
3) not the absence of fear, but not giving up when the going gets rough and the outcome seems hopeless.

This is a true story about a man my father encountered in the Absorka Mountains of Montana. Mike Minetti was an Italian immigrant who came to the United States to work on the railroad. When an accident mangled one leg, he could no longer work. After he recovered enough to get around on one crutch, he retreated to the mountains where he built a rough cabin. He lived there alone with a few goats and subsisted off the land like an Italian Euell Gibbons.

My father noticed a huge grizzly hide that covered the side of the cabin and asked Mike about it. This is Mike's story.

"One day, my goats, shesa make alotta noise, shesa scared. I looka out to see whatsa matter and dat ol' bear, hesa standin' right over there, thinkin' hesa gonna have a goat pickanick. Dose goats, shesa runna inna da house when I opena door. I grabba my gun, shesa only gotta tree bullets, but dat bear, hesa notta gonna eata my goats or Ol' Mike, no! I shoota dat bear. Hesa fall down—SPLAT! I slamma da door and wait. One day, the goats shesa shaken', Ol' Mike, hesa shakin'! Two day, the goats still ashakin', Ol' Mike still ashakin! Tree day, I peeka out. The leetle cheepmonkeys, desa crawlin' on data bear. Hesa dead!"

My father looked at Mike's very rusty .22 rifle and noticed the bent barrel. Grizzlies are notoriously hard to kill and a .22 usually only irritates them. An irritated grizzly bear is a very dangerous animal! Just one of Mike's bullets had hit the bear—right in the eye, penetrating its brain, killing it instantly. That Mike had even hit the bear with that poor excuse of a gun was a miracle.

Mike admitted he was scared. He knew the danger of a wounded or angry grizzly. His actions had all the elements of courage: 1) inner strength to withstand hardship, 2) presence of mind in the face of great odds, 3) not an absence of fear, but not giving up when the outcome seemed hopeless.

I don't expect that any of us will be face to face with a grizzly bear any time soon, but remember; courage is not the absence of fear. It is persisting when the going gets rough or the outcome seems hopeless. When you face your own "grizzly bear", or maybe a teddy bear, remember Mike Minetti and his crooked rifle.

THATSA COURAGE!

JoLynne

ANGEL IN COWBOY BOOTS

One of the wise men struggled to keep his paper crown fastened in a circle. A shepherd kept stepping on the rope that attempted to keep his bathrobe from dragging on the floor. Another shepherd swung his staff like a bat, sometimes connecting with another pageant performer, causing wails and tears. Chaos reigned in the fellowship hall.

"I'm a wise guy and you two are my helpers," announced one royally clad munchkin.

"We're wise MEN, and not your assistants," protested the studious looking wise man whose crown kept slipping over his eyes.

"Stop chasing the angel," screeched a mother, whose son antagonized the little pony-tailed blond in gossamer wings.

"Okay, we're ready, I think. Let's go," ordered the director. "Michael, that is a chalice, not a trumpet," she chastised one of the magi.

The third wise man wound the music box key of the *treasure chest*, again, and the group straggled out to the tinkling melody of "Feelings."

The children marched to their places in the church to long-familiar Christmas carols. The angel took her place on the cloth-draped milk crate, exposing her scuffed cowboy boots. She declared, "Do not fear," to the shepherds as they made their appearance in their rope-bound headdresses, carrying makeshift shepherds' crooks.

The reluctant innkeeper stumbled over his trailing robe and growled, "No room in the inn."

Mary nearly forgot to keep the Baby hidden in her robe until after she and Joseph took their places behind the manger.

A large foil star jerkily rose over the manger as the three wise men jostled their way down the aisle, still vying for 'head wise guy'. The biggest visitor from the East, the one who had harassed the angel earlier, shoved his way forward, knocking the smallest shepherd off the chancel step. She hit the floor with a pronounced *thunk*, followed by muffled sobs.

The angel leaped off her perch, stomped on the wise man's sneaker and hissed, "Meanie!" She gathered the weeping shepherd in her arms, rocking and crooning, "It's okay, honey, Jesus loves you and so do I."

To cover the moans of the culprit, who was hopping about holding his sore foot, the pianist began a rousing chorus of "*Hark the Herald Angels.*"

Once again, an angel, this one in cowboy boots, announced the Good News.

JoLynne

FLOATING IN THE AIR

Shattered, confused, I listened to the News.
I glared at the big TV screen,
Stunned, shocked, ready to scream.
Oh my God! Every, every word pierced
Into soft soil of my soul.

Now the streets flooded with flowers,
And masses of people, crowds, crowds.
Here stood the Palace, before admired,
Now was looked upon with doubts.
Pale English faces, clean-washed by fog,
Today were spotted with tears, clouded with thoughts.
Today they yearned to know the truth
Though the truth was floating in the air.

Princess was killed, Princess of the World!!!
Shocked, choked, bursting in tears,
Human races of the Earth could not,
They could not find a right word.
Though the truth was floating in the air,
Floating in the air around the earth . . .

Tatiana

ME AND ORIOLE

Oriole entered the family at two years old in Darmstadt, Germany. Dad was stationed there for a two year tour but asked for an extension when he and my stepmother, Belle, decided to adopt. They didn't ask how I felt about it. Since my new high school friends were rotating back to the states, I didn't want to stay another year in Germany and I sure didn't want to have to baby sit any two year old brats. I was perfectly content to be the only child in this family.

But I'm getting ahead of myself. I should go back to when I was still a little kid and Dad was stationed in Kansas at Ft. Riley.

My Ma died when I was eight. They told me she died of "sick kidneys", but I figured out it was from all the wine and vodka she drank.

Dad sent me to live with Grannie Mae until he married Belle two years later. Granny Mae had been strict, but I think she really loved me. Still I was glad to get back to Dad.

Belle was hard to figure. She was sure no movie star. I couldn't see what Dad saw in her. She looked more like Whoopy Goldberg than Diana Ross. She hung on Dad like she was afraid I'd take him away from her. She wasn't mean to me but I could tell she wasn't thrilled to be my second Mama. She looked old to me but claimed to be three years younger than Dad. They were married about two-and-a-half years when Dad asked me how I'd like to have a baby brother or sister. Back then I said "okay."

He said, "Belle and I hope to have a child."

He didn't tell me she was already three and a half months preggies. I found out when I came home from school a few days later and nobody was home. She had gone to the hospital. Dad brought her home the next morning. I never saw him look so sad, not even when Ma died. He told me just that "Belle lost our baby."

I was only going on ten but I knew that babies grow inside a woman's belly.

Things weren't too good after that. Belle complained a lot. They argued over lots of stuff, sometimes over me 'cause Belle said I didn't eat right and I sassed her and I was "to lazy to fart." Mostly they argued over Dad never asking for leave and staying long hours at the Supply office on Post. He was the First Sergeant for his company and hoping for another promotion.

Belle hardly ever talked to me about anything that mattered so it was unusual when she asked me, after I'd finished my homework, to sit down with her for a minute.

"Sairee," she said (she only used my nickname when she wanted to be extra nice), "you're going to have to take care of your Dad for a few days while I go to the hospital. Can you do that?"

"Sure, Mom. What's wrong? Are you sick? Is it bad?"

She said, "I'll be okay. It's not bad like your Ma's was. They're going to have to take out my female parts."

"No shit! Can you die from that?"

"Don't use gutter language. No you don't die, you just can't have more babies. I want you to keep the house clean and the dishes washed and make sure Dad sits down to supper. I'll put some things in the freezer that you can heat in the oven. You'll have to start the oven when you get home from school so things will be ready to eat when he comes home. I'll probably be away for three days."

That's all she said except that the operation was set for the following Wednesday. She didn't know how thrilled I was at the thought that I'd have Dad to myself for three whole days and I was to "take care" of him.

The time passed all too quickly. Dad came home on time each evening and we ate supper together. He told me that we were going to Germany even before he told Belle. He checked on her at the hospital over his lunch hour so he could be home after work.

He told Belle about his new assignment when she got out of the hospital. She was happy and excited about it. She'd never been out of the country.

There weren't so many arguments as they got ready to travel. We were scheduled to go just after school let out. I was thirteen that June.

Dad took on his new job like nothing else mattered. Again there were arguments about his long hours at work. Belle became more and more critical and suspicious. I overheard her accuse him of "fooling around" one night when he came home extra late. Their voices got louder.

"Dammit, Belle. I'm trying to make rank. You know the Army's about the only place a poor black boy from south Georgia stands a chance of making something of hisself."

"I think you married me just to clean your house and raise Sairetia. You don't care about my feeling at all. I think you're glad I can't have a child of my own."

Dad's voice broke. "That's not true, Belle. More than anything, I wanted the child we lost."

The words got soft then and I couldn't tell what they were saying even though they continued talking a long time, maybe even after I was asleep.

The next day Belle went to the Army Community Center and came home with stuff all about adopting in Germany.

You see, lots of black soldiers make babies while they're stationed there. They don't always marry the baby's mother. Those half-black babies aren't exactly welcome in lots of German families and they wind up put in orphanages.

Anyway, that's where Oriole comes in. Only she wasn't called "Oriole" in the orphanage. Her name we Gisele.

Dad took me along when he and Belle went to meet her for the first time. I've got to admit she was a cute little threat to my "only child" status. Her skin was the color of molasses taffy and smooth as cream. Her enormous round dark eyes weren't missing a thing. They seem to overwhelm her tiny nose and the thumb firmly caught in her little red mouth. Her hair wasn't nappy. It lay in shiny black ringlets like a cap on her head. Even as she pulled on her thumb her dimples decorated each cheek. She was not quite fat, but "plump" isn't far off.

Dad said, "She doesn't look like a Gisele."

The orphanage attendant who had brought her out asked her to say "Guten tag," which means "Good day." When she did, the words came out as a sort of chirp.

Belle said, "She sounds like a bird. Is she part blackbird?"

Dad responded, "No, she's more special. She must be an oriole. I think that would be a good name for her."

That settled it on the spot. We called her nothing else after that.

Belle had been sitting in an armchair when Oriole was brought into the room. Dad was standing. He knelt down to Oriole's height where she stood. I took his cue and squatted beside him. Belle quickly pushed out of the chair to the other side of Dad.

Oriole looked at the three of us as Dad stretched out his arms. I was startled to feel her arms hugging me instead of Dad or Belle. I felt sorry for Belle when I saw the look of pained disappointment cross her face. My own amazement grew as I allowed a flush of deep pleasure wash through me at having this little person target me for her first hug.

That's how it came about that at fourteen I became sort of the *real* mother to Oriole. Try as she might, Belle couldn't succeed in making a mother's bond with Oriole. My own need to have someone love me responded to Oriole's same feelings. We shared Dad's precious time at home. I surprised myself that I didn't really mind sharing. Somehow she *added to* instead of *taking away* the time with him.

Belle lost out all the way around. I guess she resented my connection to Oriole because she was on my case for any little thing. Eventually she left us and she and Dad divorced, but I'll have to talk about that some other time. Right now I have to take Oriole to choir practice. Her bird chirps are sounding more like a songbird every day. I think she'll grow up to be in the movies.

Mary

A FRIEND

I have a friend
With long dark hair,
Sparkling eyes
And a funny hat

She smiles a lot
But doesn't say why
And when I ask,
She looks at the sky

And then she said
What fun it was
To watch the clouds
Just passing by . . .

I looked at her
Wondering why
I shouldn't watch
Clouds in the sky

And may be then,
I would smile a lot,
Just like my friend
With a funny hat!

Lana

THE CANDY MAN

Nearly fourteen years ago, Johnny started his new job at the Naco port of entry. Prior to three weeks before moving to the area, he had never heard of Naco, Arizona. It wasn't even on the map he had. But here he was, starting a new career as a U. S. Customs Inspector in his mid-forties. Before this new job, he had been employed in the school system as an educator, a career counselor, and an administrator. An army career was his plans after high school. However, after three years of active duty, marriage, and two young children, his career direction changed and he decided going back to school. Now, after a number of years in education, he was ready for another change in career.

His new job was certainly different from being in the classroom, but with some similarities. He was working with people. There were rules or laws requiring compliance, and he found there was the politics in the system to contend with. Johnny liked his job, but not the politics. Hopefully things will work out well.

Working on the line consists of checking vehicles and passengers crossing the border both ways. Most of the northbound vehicles are occupied by the Hispanic population of Mexico and people from further south of the border. Many do not like or are fearful of the *"aduana"* the men in uniform at the port of entry. Johnny discovered that even in a small town with a small port, the challenges can be most difficult. He also found out it's not what you know or your educational background that counts most. Sometimes, it's not even your job performance that gives you "Brownie" points, but who you know and who you cater to that counts.

Johnny grew up in a family of limited means and where he often felt deprived. On several occasions, as a youngster, he lived with his grandparents or other relatives due to the instability at home. Much of his clothes were hand-me-downs. He wore shoes stuffed with toilet paper at the toes to fit. Mostly, he walked around barefeet. On occasion, he wore slippers.

Once, when he found a whole dollar bill walking home from school, he was so excited but scared and didn't tell anyone. Instead, he went to the little neighborhood grocery store he passes by. This time, instead of just looking in and drooling at the large jars of candies he saw on the counter, he went in and purchased a little bag of candies. He was thrilled especially when he even received a few coins back. Out the door he went, while reaching in the bag of candies and plopped one in his mouth after removing the wrapper.

"Oooh, yummy, this is soo good!" he thought with a grin on his face as he slowly walked home.

Halfway home and after devouring most of the candies, he decided to get rid of his change so his Mom would not find any money on him. Seeing a bush nearby, he threw the coins under the bush and continued walking without looking back.

Now, a father of five children, his need for candies has long been satisfied, but still enjoys an occasional sweet. He finds great satisfaction in his work, but it can be most stressful at times.

He enjoyed the children walking across, talking to them about school and their experiences. He was glad and encouraged them to continue their good works. He also started giving them lollipops whenever they shared their accomplishments with him. The children were grateful and looked forward to sharing their schoolwork and experiences with him. Though sometimes only brief, he enjoyed their encounters also.

Johnny had candies in one of his pockets every day. One day, a toddler in a car, probably just over a year old, was fussy and crying while his mother tried to hold him. It was obvious that the family had traveled quite a distance to get to the border. Two other children in the back seat were restless and starting to whine at times. Even the parents looked tired.

The father told his little son to stop crying. Then he turned and told the older children that the *"aduana"* would take them away if they didn't behave.

This annoyed Johnny because it only made the children more fearful of him. The toddler cried louder. The other children hid their faces with their hands.

"Senor, por favor, do not tell your children that. I will not take them away. You only scare them more when you say that." Then he continued, *"Por favor, Senor, con permiso, may I give your children some palleto?"*

"*Ah, si, Senor, si,*" the father replied with a more relaxed expression. His wife smiled as Johnny reached into his pocket. Turning to the crying toddler, he told him in a somewhat gruff voice to stop crying, and showed the little one the candy while smiling. The toddler looked at him rather frightened at first but started to grin and rub his eyes when he saw the lollipop.

The older children stared at the inspector the whole time wondering if he would give them a lollipop also.

Johnny then turned and looked at the children in the back seat, grinned, then pulled out more lollipops. The children's once fearful expressions turned into full smiles as he handed each one a candy.

"*Gracias, Senor, gracias. Bye, bye,*" said the children with delight as they started opening their candy wrappers.

"*Mucho gracias, mui amable,*" said the mother.

"*Gracias, mucho gracias,*" called out the father as he drove pass the smiling inspector.

Inspite of all the problems and challenges the rest of the day, Johnny continued to share the candies in his pocket to the children he felt needed a lift.

A warm and happy feeling engulfed him. He went home that day and asked his wife to purchase more lollipops and other wrapped candies to have in his pocket whenever he worked on the line. It didn't take long for him to became known as the "Candy Man" or the *"Palleta Aduana."* Some of his co-workers even called him that at times. The work environment improved as the staff became more pleasant to work with and the people passing through were usually friendlier and smiled more.

As days and years passed and the *"Palleta Aduana"* developed a special bonding with the children and their families. Even after retiring, they greet him and many talk to him updating him on their lives whenever and wherever they see him. Though work was difficult, most challenging and highly stressful at times, the "Candy Man" developed lasting friendships and found gladness in his job.

Loretta

BOVINE BALLADEER

Clem Weyland was a little nuts; no, he was a lot nuts. To be honest, his name would fit on several pages of the psychiatric diagnostic manual. He was an odd boy, the one that often got picked on in school. He became even more odd after his Timothy O'Leary decade of "playing around with drugs," as he put it.

He was no longer troubled by neighbors or teased by the teenagers in the area, once they realized he imagined persecutors behind every tree. When he was having one of his severe paranoid episodes, Clem's conspiracy convictions caused him to climb to the roof of his house and spray the area with weapons fire; shot-gun, M16, AK47, whatever guns he grabbed from his collected arsenal. The ground and trees around his house were pockmarked with evidence of his war against those plotting against him. It was a good thing his acreage put plenty of distance between him and the nearest neighbors. He was convinced the military, FBI, CIA, Sheriff's Department and the Border Patrol were conspiring to drive him crazy so they could steal his land for a spaceship-landing site.

The aging hippie/cowboy lived in the house that sat in the middle of 750 acres he inherited from his parents. Clem had never held a regular job, at least not for long, and spent his time compulsively cleaning. He knew within an eighth of an inch if something was out of its assigned place. Dust didn't dare enter his house. Between cleaning frenzies, he took showers, often several a day, and he planned what fortifications he would build next.

These battlements he obsessively envisioned never materialized. Clem would get so far as to hire a neighbor with a Caterpillar tractor to scoop out holes for footings or foundations and would have truckloads of bagged cement delivered. His property was dotted with huge holes on the edge of which were mounds of the stacked bags, solidified in the weather and useless. It was a wonder some of his cattle didn't fall into the holes with resulting broken legs.

That's one thing Clem did, and did well; raise cattle, his source of income. Somehow his psychosis seemed to have no influence over his cattleman's savvy and he prospered with his small herd.

Clem's other untainted ability was singing. He had a beautiful, smooth tenor voice. He sang extremely well the one song he knew, and his only audience was his cattle. Every day, as he forked hay to them from the back of his pickup, he sang to them. It was probably the most unconditional approval he'd had in his life.

One day he noticed eight of his cattle were missing and went in search of them. He finally spotted a place where the fence had been cut, then repaired. Upon closer examination he could see hoof marks starting on his side of the fence and continuing on the other side, stopping where tire tracks began. Rustlers!

Clem had an on-going conflict with Chuck, a neighboring rancher. They had been boys together, and Chuck was one of Clem's tormentors in school. He felt sure the cattle would be found on Chuck's property, so he promptly drove there to confront the old thief. After a lengthy heated exchange, Chuck demanded, "Prove it!"

Brands weren't bothered with much anymore, so proving ownership of feeder cattle was a little difficult. The two men, accompanied by two of Chuck's hired men, drove out to where the cattle were cleaning up their morning's ration of hay. Clem climbed into the back of the pickup and started to sing.

"Retorna me, cara mia ti amo. Solo tu, solo tu, mio cuore."

Heads of cattle raised. They stared at Clem and then went back to gathering the last of breakfast. That is, all except for eight steers who separated themselves from the herd and trotted over to the pickup.

"Well, I'll be damned," Chuck said in amazement. "Boys, load 'em up and take 'em back."

That was the last time any of Clem's cattle were rustled. Maybe it was because his cattle were the only ones who understood Italian.

"Return to me, my dear, I love you. Only you, only you, my heart."

JoLynne

COURAGE OF A DIFFERENT COLOR

"What's this one for, Grappa, the one down in the corner, the one that is half brown?"

The boy, now showing strong signs of the man he will become, was always interested in the display case that held his grandfather's military medals. They had enjoyed the times together when the boy pointed out a particular medal, and said, "Tell me about this one, Grappa!"

"Well, son, that little medal is a unit medal and the one I'm most proud of, even more than these up here," he answered, pointing to the Purple Heart and the Medal of Honor at the top of the case.

"You see, that was the one I felt I really earned. It was like this. We were ordered to the unit meeting just before we were discharged. In our last battle, only eleven of us were carried out still breathing, and only seven of us lived to make it to that meeting. Five of us were in wheelchairs and the other two were on crutches, in the first row below the speaker's platform. The Colonel blathered on and on about body count and the glory of 'victory.' It made us all feel sicker than we already were.

"Everyone was so numbed by the officer's drone that no one noticed the wheelchair working it's way up the ramp at the side of the platform. All were frozen with revulsion when the Colonel said, 'It is too bad these troops can't stand up here and receive these medals, looking me in the eye like men,' waving the handful of medals in the air.

"Just then the wheelchair reached the officer's side and the man in it struggled with obvious agonized effort to stand on his feet. There was not a sound from anyone as he turned to face the Colonel.

'With all *due* respect, *Sir!* You can take your medals and shove them up your ass.'

"With an explosive sound, everyone in the room stood up, cheering, including those in the Colonel's entourage. Even those in the wheelchairs struggled up. The two men who had no legs at all were lifted up by those comrades closest to them. "Son, it wasn't until our first reunion that we found out that all of us had painted half of that medal brown!"

JoLynne

KATRINA

At five a.m. disaster struck,
Katrina came, knocking at our door!
We tried to stop her with all our might,
But, full of rage, she pushed us aside
She slammed the door and cursed us all,
Broke all the windows and flooded the hall,

She breached the levies,
Upturned the cars,
Flooded the houses
And wiped them out . . .

Thousands of people have lost their homes,
Priceless possessions and all they owned,
Many have drowned in that awful flood,
At the time when Katrina came to our door.

Lana

AN OLD COWPOKE WENT RIDIN' OUT

"Pappy, get those cows away from the house! I can't grow so much as a darned dandelion if you can't keep them away. Did you hear me? Pappy, Pappy?"

"Yes, yes, Annabelle? I heard you. Just let me get my hat."

The old man pushed himself out of the chair at his desk and made his way to the rack by the door where his hard-used everyday Stetson hung over a nail. He dutifully plodded to the west of the house and shooed three young cows off to the range beyond the small plot designated for a front yard to the house. The barbed wire fencing lay on the ground beside a post that had slumped over after the previous night's rain. He pulled the post upright before heading to a shed that contained odd equipment; retuning with a shovel to secure the post in place. He packed dirt around its base and added several inches more that he tamped down with multiple blows of the back of the shovel. He paused a moment to regain his breath while leaning on the tool before taking to the shed and stowing it carefully.

Once inside again, he replaced his hat in its proper spot and turned toward the bathroom to clean up from his labor.

"Pappy! What are you doing? What kept you so long? Why do you make me worry so?"

"I'm sorry, Dear. I have to wash up. I had to secure a fence post and got pretty dirty."

"Well, get on in here. Our lunch is ready to eat and the coffee's hot. You know I don't like it to get cold.

"I'll be right there. Don't wait. I'm coming."

He sat down at the TV table placed in front of his favorite chair. A bowl of beef stew and a mug of coffee awaited. Annabelle was already spooning her portion from where she sat facing the large window. She had a lap robe covering her knees.

"Pappy, would you mind turning the heat up? I've been cold ever since it rained and this place just doesn't get warm enough."

He obligingly lifted his table forward to make more room to raise up, and went to the wall thermostat to change the setting. He had to lean far back in place and turn his head to one side in order to read the numbers of the dial. The stoop of his spine was so extreme that a view of his own boots was what he saw most of the time.

When he finished the stew he announced, "The mail should be up by now, so I'm going to drive into town to pick it up. Is there anything you want while I'm out?"

"You know they charge too much at the Rodeo Grocery. Besides, we got everything we need yesterday in Douglas."

"Does that mean you don't want anything?"

"Well, you could get me the Range News. I haven't seen it for a while."

The trip to the town of approximately two hundred souls was less than a mile. The old man was greeted with smiles in the new little U S Office. "Hey, Ned. How are things going for You?"

"Well, okay I guess. I don't get around as good as I used to and it takes longer to get things done."

"Sounds like you've got a touch of *senioritis*. It gets a lot of us these days."

The cowboy who spoke looked to be about fifty-six or so. Ned didn't count that to be "senior" anything. He had still been ridin', ropin', and wrangling' in his fifties, but after he was thrown off his horse last year, he'd had to settle for ridin' his pickup truck. The doc told him that at eighty-five he had no business making some poor horse take him all over God's creation. So these days he left it to his *vaquero* Guadalupe to bring the cattle where the pickup couldn't go.

The Postmistress asked, "How is Annabelle?"

Ned shook his head. "She's not doing too good. She has an appointment with a doctor in Silver City next week. He should tell us what we're dealing with then."

"I'm sorry to hear that, and that's a long drive, you take care, hear?"

"Thanks. I sure will."

Walking out, he glanced at the envelopes in his hand. With his deteriorating vision, he could only make out the largest print without a magnifying glass. One very large envelope was boldly addressed to "Edward and Annabelle Hall." He recognized it as coming from his attorney in Lordsburg. They had recently met with him to formalize their wills. Most of Ned's assets were in land holdings. He had been selling off his leases and reducing his herd over a period of years. He kept only about two hundred head now, enough to get by with only one regular hired had.

Annabelle enthusiastically engaged in multiple money-making schemes since their marriage thirteen years before. She had converted one small residence he owned into a Bed and Breakfast and sold it at a small profit. Feeling encouraged by her success, she turned another small town lot into a self-storage yard, again selling at a profit. The house he brought her to after they married became uncomfortable for her due to having too many near neighbors, so he purchased a large pre-manufactured home and had it moved out to their present location on the ranch. The town house was sold at a satisfying return. Always seeking change, Annabelle was currently determined to build a house of her own design. She submitted her design to a professional architect and it was even now being constructed an eighth of a mile away.

Ned had survived two previous wives. The bride of his youth died young. He never spoke of her. His second wife, Lupe Tellez, suffered severe emotional problems, to the extent that Ned hired a fulltime, live-in caretaker for her until Lupe passed away in 1981.

Many who knew Ned over time, were mystified by his choice of the wife of his sunset years. They presented a startling contrast—he was soft-spoken, she often strident. He was rarely critical—she was strongly opinionated. He followed set patterns and settled ways—she favored continual change. Her outspokenness often alienated others.

Nevertheless, Ned was drawn to her strong independent streak, her disregard of convention, and her determination to live life on her terms. Ned, too, had resolved, long before meeting Annabelle, to live life on his own terms. His mother married a rancher, but hated the ranch life. She loved socializing and owning pretty things. She reared Ned in Los Angeles society, sending him for summers on the ranch with his father, until he rebelled in his late teens and returned to the ranch permanently. The son of western pioneers, Ned felt himself part of the land he loved.

When he was on his way home from his mail run, he saw the construction contractor's vehicle at the building site and turned on the access road to have word with him.

"Howdy, Mr. Hall. How are you?"

"Fine, just fine. When do you think you'll be able to get the walls up?"

"The units are to be delivered tomorrow. I think the rain's passed on so we should be able to get right to work. With any luck we'll have you in your new home by Thanksgiving."

"Good. My wife will be glad to hear that. She gets more anxious by the day."

The house was ready by Thanksgiving, complete with a blue ceiling and deeper blue walls in the hexagonal-sided living/dining room. In spite of hiring helpers for the move, both Ned and Annabelle were exhausted by the effort. Though genuinely thrilled with her dream realized, Annabelle was unable to reclaim her usual energy and by Spring had not started any fresh projects. Her norm was to have no less than four projects going at once.

A second visit to the doctor in Silver City confirmed his tentative diagnosis from before. Annabelle had pancreatic cancer, which was inoperable. The heavy narcotics supplied to her as the pain increased tempered her sharp tongue.

"Pappy, you know you are the dearest man in the world, don't you?"

"Now, I wouldn't say that."

"Don't argue with me. You are, and I know it, and I'll tell the world it's true."

"Well, now, whatever you say, Annabelle."

"Pappy, what year was it that they elected you to the Cowboy Hall of Fame in Wilcox?"

"I don't rightly recall. I think it was six or seven years ago."

"Well, I just love that portrait they painted of you. It made me so proud."

Annabelle never explained why she chose to call him "Pappy." He'd never been anyone's parent and she was six years his senior. If he took exception to the pet name, he never let on.

The disease claimed its price. She became increasingly invalid and Ned sustained his loving devotion to her care to the very end. She died on October 13, 2003.

The funeral was held graveside in the little country cemetery overlooking the ranch and the community. Ned's friends turned out to support him and pay respects. He spared no expense. Included in the contract was a waterproof grave liner to contain the casket. Ned insisted on staying after the guests had all gone, to see the casket lowered. To his great dismay, the gravediggers had not allowed for the extra dimensions of the liner and the whole thing would not fit. The attendants cranked the casket back up, went for shovels in their panel vehicle, and came back to dig their way out of the dilemma.

It was a sight to behold—three mortuary attendants in dark business suits shoveling at the corners of the open grave. Two of Ned's friends remained at his side to see him through the stressful moments. A fresh attempt was made to lower the casket to no avail. Hacking at the hard soil and shoveling resumed. The third try to put Annabelle to rest resulted in the coffin being jammed halfway down. This time the funeral supervisor stepped into the pit on top of the coffin and, using all of his considerable body weight, jumped up and down until gradually the box was in place. With each hard thump, Ned visibly winced. With the final *WHAUMP!* Ned wryly remarked, "She didn't want to go."

Never one to linger in the past, Ned went on with his daily ranch chores. Prolonged shortfall of rain saw the land in drought condition. When occasional rain came it didn't linger long enough to sustain the germinating grasses. Ned and Guadalupe were pressed to buy feed and distribute it to the cattle out on the range. Animals pushed against vulnerable fencing trying to reach nibbles of grass outside its limits. The men constantly monitored the fences.

They rounded up the herd and split out thirty or so head to haul to market. Ned considered selling off all the stock but couldn't quite bring himself to that irrevocable step. He approached his one-time old partner Scotty with a proposition.

"Friend, how about you buying my animals and just leave them on my range until you're ready to sell them?"

Scotty had long since passed his most virile watershed, not quite as old as Ned, and still ramrod straight, yet finding it hard to marshal the energy needed to keep his own spread profitable.

"Ned, old partner, I've given it a lot of thought and I have to say 'Thanks, but no thanks.' Hauling feed and hauling water is already taking the starch out of me. I just can't take on any more. No hard feelings, I hope?"

"Of course not. I understand. It's just that I'm finding it a little hard to keep up with things. I don't move around so good and I don't always see what needs doing."

So Ned kept on. Among his closet friends he allowed that he really missed the companionship of Annabelle. One of those who knew the couple well was Bill Cavaliere, former Sheriff of Hidalgo County, New Mexico. He assisted Ned with arrangements for the service at Annabelle's funeral. Bill and his wife Jill were especially appreciative of Ned and Annabelle because they had set up college trust funds for the Cavalieres' son and daughter. Though they lived a distance away, in Animas, New Mexico, Bill tried to check on Ned from time to time, as did a few other friends. There were no relatives to show any concern for his well being.

A year passed uneventfully and cold weather prevailed on the high desert. Ned's restricted driver's license was withdrawn pending a new eye exam. He was forced to limit his driving to the ranch and essential trips for groceries and supplies. He made it a policy not to attempt driving after dark.

On the Sunday afternoon of November 28, 2004, Bill Cavaliere received a call from Guadalupe. Ned had not attended the morning mass at the little Mission San Felipe in Rodeo. He never missed service unless he was ill or out of town. His habit was to attend the protestant Bible study group after mass was over. He sought to support God's work wherever he could. Guadalupe had gone to the house and Ned was not there. His pickup was gone. He wanted to know if perhaps Ned was visiting Bill's family. He wasn't.

Other close friends were called. No one had seen him. Guadalupe was the last to speak to him on Saturday morning when they discussed work needing attention for the week ahead. Saturday night a heavy rainstorm passed through the region.

Bill organized a search party. He rallied his friends and the new county sheriff. He contacted the Border Patrol and the State Highway Patrols for both New Mexico and Arizona. The Border Patrol engaged their surveillance helicopter to broaden the search. Monday and Tuesday passed without results. The Saturday storm left the land muddy and bitter cold at night. Wednesday Guadalupe was out on horseback, again searching the trails on the ranch. He found Ned's body, but his employer, benefactor, and friend had gone from this life.

The searchers that remained located the pickup truck deeply stuck in the mud three and a half miles from where Ned's dark night walk ended. They speculated he was intent on reaching Guadalupe's bunk house to ask for his help. It was no more than a quarter of a mile away from where he stopped. The Medical Examiner later reported that his great heart had given out.

Services in Mission San Felipe were held on the sixth of December. There was standing room only. The same afternoon a memorial service took place in the Rodeo Community Hall. Over one hundred and fifty people gathered and the ladies provided a ranch-hand chuck wagon meal to feed everyone. Some folks had an extra piece of pie "for Ned."

What had called him out on that miserable winter night remains a mystery. Perhaps he heard a calf bawling. Perhaps he worried about a downed fence. Perhaps he hoped to divert some of the heavy rain to fill a dry watering hole. Whatever the case, he was a rancher to the last and was wearing his old Stetson and his boots to meet his maker.

Mary

A LESSON IN JUDGING

Most of us have developed holiday traditions by habit if not intentionally. We use familiar decorations, have the same foods and eat our holiday meal or watch the football game about the same time every year. But what happens when something interrupts that traditional pattern? One Christmas season the traditions of our family were disrupted with a profound and lasting effect.

Our family tradition was to attend the morning church service and then go home to our holiday dinner on Christmas Day. One year when my children were small, we went to church as usual. We heard the familiar story, sang all the carols, and were ready to go home to our turkey dinner. The pastor stopped us as we were leaving the church to ask if we could give a man a ride. He had just been discharged from a nearby hospital and had no way to get home. My husband agreed without knowing any details. We were introduced to our passenger, a scruffy and unpleasantly aromatic, unkempt Native American man, one arm in a sling and a tattered brown paper bag clutched with the other. He told us he needed a ride to Jemez Pueblo, over an hour's drive from our home in Albuquerque. There went our usual Christmas Day! He agreed to have dinner with us before we took him home. At least we wouldn't miss our dinner.

As I was sandwiched between our odiferous hitchhiker and my husband in our small car, the Christmas spirit drained away as I became increasingly irritated at the change in our plans. After we got home to holiday aromas and I began the final preparations for our meal, our guest asked if he could use the bathroom. Forty-five minutes later, the gravy was congealing, the rolls were cold and the ice in the glasses was melting. He was still in the bathroom. In my judgmental irritation, I imagined him passed out from drinking out of his brown paper bag or having done something drastic with my husband's straight-edged razor. Just as I was about to ask my husband to check on him, he came out. He had showered, shaved and struggled into the clean shirt he had carried in his paper bag.

While we shared our dinner, Teddy explained he had been out herding sheep for a week when his horse had stepped into a gopher hole, throwing him. His brothers brought him into the Indian Hospital where he was hospitalized with a dislocated shoulder and concussion. A snowstorm had just begun and they needed to get back to get their sheep into shelter, so they had dropped him off at the hospital. A spare shirt was all he had with him. Because they had no phone, he had no way to let his family know he was ready to go home.

As you may have guessed, I was feeling ashamed of how quick I had been to assume the worst. I was receiving a sharp lesson in how being prejudiced and judgmental can ruin enjoyment of a very special season.

However, the story and the lesson didn't end there. The trip to the Pueblo went quickly as Teddy shared stories about a way of life very different from ours. It was a clear, bright, very cold day. We arrived just in time to see the entire village assembling in the square near the kiva. Teddy asked us to stay as guests of his family to observe the Deer Dances, which are part of his holiday tradition. Because of the cold, we were given warm, bright blankets to wrap up in. I stood with the women from Teddy's family, my husband joined the men and our two children joined a semi-circle of Jemez children. I have a very vivid and heart-warming memory of seeing my two towheads among all the black haired ones.

After the dances, Teddy insisted we join his family for their traditional meal. After sharing their spicy mutton stew and hominy, each member of the family came to us, one by one, to thank us for bringing home their uncle or brother. With the presentation of a loaf of bread freshly baked in the family beehive oven, Teddy and his family said goodbye as we headed back to Albuquerque to resume our own traditions.

The generosity and gratitude of a family who overlooked my prejudice and the grudging nature of my hospitality overwhelmed me. They shared all that they had and gently, if unintentionally, reminded me of the reason for the season and the purpose behind the traditions. Recalling that experience became part of our holidays. My daughter shares that indelible memory with her students every year.

What can happen when your holiday traditions and plans are disrupted? Do you get frantic and irritable? You may find your judgments and prejudices being challenged. You may also experience a whole new approach to the spirit of the season. Perhaps you won't need as pointed a lesson as I did. Let yourself be open and you may have an extra-special holiday, too!

JoLynne

A PRECIOUS LITTLE BABY

We came upon a baby,
A twinkle in her eyes,
She smiled a little crooked smile,
A tear dropped from my eyes.

We saw this precious baby,
She stole our hearts away,
We knew that soon she'd be our baby,
One we've been praying for each day.

We held this precious little one
Into our eyes she gazed.
The warmest feelings in our hearts,
Thank you, Lord, we praised.

I hugged this awesome baby,
Her warm, soft, small hands upon my face,
She'll no longer be without a mother,
And a father to love and embrace.

We love this precious baby,
Together we will learn and grow.
Already, a part of our family she's become,
Joyfulness we found and will come to really know.

Loretta

ELMORE MITCHELL, WHERE ARE YOU?

"Elmore Mitchell, where are you? Or more to the point, how are you?"

These questions didn't trouble her mind all the time or even often, but once in a while they would be there, intruding on whatever she was attending to at the moment. She wondered if Elmore felt the tie between them as strongly as she did. That tie seemed amazingly strong to her, in spite of the fact that she only vaguely remembered he was from somewhere in the South, maybe Arkansas, was single and had no children. She could only guess at his age, possible mid-thirties. It is surprising how strong a tie can be forged between two people who have never met and had only one brief telephone conversation, a connection molded out of the events of brief seconds.

The lead vehicle, a pickup camper, of their three-car caravan took the freeway exit at a reasonable speed. The other two cars lagged a little behind, waiting for the two parallel semis to pass. In a surreal way, she knew there was going to be a collision. She didn't expect it to be in the median. The driver of the pickup and the driver of the inside semi simultaneously made the same accident-avoiding decision to go into the median.

The semi was undamaged. The pickup cab and left front corner of the camper were crushed. The driver and the boy in that corner died instantly. Another boy was thrown out, seriously injured. The other three boys were badly shaken, but essentially unharmed.

An off-duty highway patrolman was jogging along the road, and summoned help with his radio. Within three minutes, the area swarmed with officers, EMTs and firemen. The whole group, eight teenagers and a female chaperone, was whisked to the nearest hospital

While the seriously injured boy was being attended to, the rest of the group utilized a hospital conference room and phones to call family. She notified her husband and then the other boy's family. When the hospital social worker asked her if there was anyone else she wished to speak to, she asked to talk to the truck driver.

The male voice on the phone was hesitant, shaky, full of anxiety and dread of what she might say. He tried to express his feelings, his condolences, his regret. Knowing that those feelings couldn't be adequately verbalized, she stopped him and asked if he was all right. He said, "I wish it was me instead, ma'am." She could only tell him that she knew the accident had been unavoidable and he had taken appropriate action, not his fault that it didn't work. He sounded relieved to hear she wasn't blaming him, holding the outcome against him. He thanked her for talking to him. That was the only time they had contact.

She had witnessed the death of her son, and the grief healed with the passing years, but once in a while, especially around the anniversary, she would wonder, "Elmore Mitchell, where are you? How are you? I hope you no longer have nightmares and have forgiven yourself."

JoLynne

MY APO

Emiliana Tolentino is my grandmother. We called her Apo. She was short, standing just under four feet ten inches tall, but she was a giant to me in courage and strength. Born in the Philippine Islands in the late 1800's, she migrated to Hawaii accompanied by a cousin, Ermo, after she was widowed with three children—a boy and two girls. Only her youngest daughter, Romana came with them at this time. Romana was 8 years old. An older brother, Aurelio, and sister, Maxima, remained in the Philippines migrating at a later time with relatives.

I remember her most when she was older, with a few soft lines across her narrow forehead. As she smiled, soft crows feet wrinkles would show at the corners of her eyes and some wrinkles on the bridge of her nose. Her face was narrow and smooth, shiny skin covered her high cheek bones. Her thinning, long, salt and pepper colored hair was combed back over her ears, tied in a knot at the back of her head, and held in place by a light brown shell comb. Her lips were thin, but smiled a broad smile. Sometimes a couple of her discolored, decaying teeth are displayed. Her shoulders were narrow and bony, her hands calloused with finger joints arthritic, and her back slightly stooped forward. Her upper arms once muscular, now with some sagging, showed evidence of strong firmness. On rare occasions, I remember her smoking a toscani, a kind of rolled up cigar, with a friend or two when they visited.

I still recall Apo carrying a 100# bag of rice on her shoulders when she was in her fifties. "Wow, she is so strong!" I thought.

Before that, on many occasions, she carried a bundle of clothes wrapped in a recycled rice bag tied in a knot balanced on top of her head while carrying my baby brother or another wrapped bundle of clothes in her arms or other things.

For a small woman, Apo's feet seemed large because they were wide. She usually wore slippers but often walked bare feet around the house. Her toes and feet were callused. Sometimes she would apply Vicks vaporub when they bothered her. Vicks was a multipurpose medicine for aches, pains, colds, and cough. She used it frequently. She hardly ever complained of anything and took things in stride, even with her arthritis, saying that this was all part of life and growing old.

Apo often wore a long, loose, white cotton camisole with wide shoulder straps, resembling a long sleeveless dress. Over it, she usually wore an above the ankle length navy blue or gray skirt tied at the waistline. This was her usual daily wear at home when it was warm. She never wore a zippered skirt. I don't think she even owned one. I don't recall seeing her wear a pair of slacks or pants. She probably never had any except when she was younger and working in the fields. On cooler days, she would wear a sweater. If there was an occasion to, like having visitors, she would dress in a pastel colored or plaid printed blouse with a collar and buttons in the front over her camisole at home. On special occasions like a holiday or a celebration, a silk blouse was in order. I believe when we were growing up, her wardrobe consisted of no more than a dozen items at any one time.

She loved her round, gold, pierced earrings and wore them all the time. Other than a silver bracelet, I don't think she owned any other jewelry.

Washdays were the only times I saw Apo's legs above her knees. Apo and her daughter, Romana, did the laundry for the single men who lived in our neighborhood. The men were hired to work for the sugar plantation by contract from the Philippines and had no family close by. Apo and Romana earned some money doing their laundry every week. The men called them "labandiras" and paid them monthly for their services. There was a saying we used to hear about payday "fifty cents an hour, four bucks a day," but I think this was what the men were paid. The "labandiras" were paid less.

The men would bring their dirty laundry usually on Saturdays, and at the same time would pick up their clean laundry that they had dropped off the previous week. There was never a lack of dirty clothes.

Working out in the sugar cane fields, their clothes were soiled with red dirt. The clothes had to be boiled in hot soapy water first to loosen the dirt. After the water had cooled down, Apo would squat over a large almost flat rock with her skirt pulled up above her knees. Her left hand turned the dirty, wet sudsy clothes. With her right hand, she pounded the clothes with a large wooden paddle which helped to remove the soil. After the pounding, the clothes were scrubbed with a brush, then rinsed in a tub of water thoroughly then hung out to dry on the clothes lines in the back yard.

There were days when clothes were not hung outside. Those were the days when nearby sugar cane fields were ready for harvest and burned. The smell of the smoke would penetrate and contaminate the area. Fragments of the burned sugar cane leaves would rise and float all over the place, including sticking to damp clothes outside. We called the burned leaves "back snow." Some days it got pretty messy.

Several years later, we had a wringer type washing machine and didn't have to rinse the clothes three or four times by hand. It was nice having the washing machine to finish the job. Once the clothes were washed, they were put through the wringer. Apo sometimes preferred to just squeeze the water from the clothes before hanging them out to dry. I think once of twice, she almost got her fingers caught in between the wringers.

Apo was soft spoken and never talkative. She spoke in her native language-the Ilocano dialect. She learned a few simple English words. "No," "ya," and "I dunno" were her most frequently used words. She always thought for a moment before answering a question. She was slow to anger. When she did get angry, you know she had a good reason, and you'd best not say anything, but just listen to her quietly until she was through talking.

Apo was never afraid of hard work. I remember her raising some pigs to help her son, Aurelio. In those days, uneaten food was saved in 5 gallon metal cans and collected from each household in the neighborhood. These were called "slop cans." After the contents were gathered by her son, Apo would boil the slop in a large container over an outdoor burning pit. When cooled, she would feed the pigs. She'd also clean the pens which was not an easy task with all different sizes of pigs running around. She always carried the rake not only to clean the pen but also to chase the pigs away from her if they got too close. Once, she nearly tripped over a baby pig which ran right in front of her squealing.

Other animals she raised during her lifetime included chickens, ducks, and rabbits.

Gardening was her favorite past time. She always had a garden and grew her favorite vegetables. We knew them by their Ilocano names—*tarong, paria, utong, camatis, lasuna, baoang, saluyot, camuteg, tabungao, kabatiti,* and *marungay* (eggplant, bittermelon, long beans, tomato, onions, garlic, okra, and a variety of squashes). Using several of these vegetables for her cooking, she made her favorite dish *"pinakbet."* *"Bagoong"* or fishsauce was her favorite flavoring for most of her cooking. We all enjoyed her pork *"adobo"* on hot rice.

On special occasions, she cooked up a large pot of coconut dessert pudding with mochi balls. It was called *"paradosdos."* I loved it's soft, smooth, but lumpy, sugary, coconut flavor. It was delicious—especially when still warm. I had never seen her use a recipe book, but her results were always flavorful and good. Whatever she cooked was usually very good.

During part of WW II and shortly after, Apo worked at the Naval Housing Area as a housekeeper. Not owning a vehicle and not knowing how to drive, she along with other women rode a vehicle provided for them to and from work traveling approximately twenty miles daily. I found a record of her payroll one day and for the year 1945, she earned an income of $1,779.94 and paid an income tax of $35.59.

By the time she was in her 90's her vision was poor. She lived with Romana who took care of her. Although practically blind and with difficulty walking, she got up everyday and received help with the activities of daily living. She walked with a cane, and sat in her favorite chair on the porch for long periods of time whenever the weather was nice and almost always she had a smile on her face. She was never forgotten by friends and family and was visited periodically. She would often be frustrated because she couldn't see well.

"Ay sos, Maria kusep, diac makakitan ken diac malaguep iti nagan mo!" she would say. *"Dispensarem, annaco,"* she added, apologizing for not being able to recognize the person or remember their names.

One day, after breakfast, she told her daughter that she was very tired of living and that she's lived a long time and felt it was time for her to go. My mother looked at her understandingly and after a silent moment replied in their native dialect, *"Ammoc nga narigat iti biag mo ta bakit kan. Na suroc nga sang nga gasot iti tawen mon. Awan iti mabalen co. Ag walo ca, Mama. Ibagam kenni Apo Dios iti riknam. Ammo na iti biag mo, ken rigat mo. Mangeg na iti walo mo."*

Apo looked her way. Slowly, thoughtfully she nodded her head. The rest of the day went by uneventful.

The next morning, Apo got up as usual. After having breakfast, she sat at the table for a short while, then went outside to sit on the porch for about an hour. When she came back in, she told her daughter, *"Nabanog accon. Innac ag giddan iti cama, Annaco."*

"Okay, Mama, I know you tiyed," Romana said and assisted her back to bed. Soon after, Apo was sound asleep.

Shortly after one o'clock, Romana wondered why Apo had not gotten up by then to have lunch and had not heard any noises from her room like usual.

Romana went to Apo's room to check on her. Apo was still in bed. As she approached the bed, she observed that Apo was no longer breathing but she had a smile on her face. Tears filled her eyes. Apo's prayers were answered. At 106 years old, Apo was where she wanted to be.

Loretta

*(Interpreted— "I know this life is hard for you because of your age. You're over a hundred years old and there's nothing I can do. Tell God how you feel. He knows your life and how hard it is now. He'll hear your prayers.")

KELLY'S TURN

Tracy pulled the car up in front of a neat stuccoed house in one of the older neighborhoods on the near south side of town. The door opened as she stepped through the low gate of the front yard.

"Hello, Mrs. Davis. Is our traveler packed and ready?"

"Ready? He's been ready for the last two days and climbing the walls 'til I'm nearly ready to hog tie him. But if you're talking about his things, they're in these two bags." She thrust two suitcases forward. One was new but of cheap material. It was provided by Child Protective Services volunteers to replace the *Safeway Luggage* in which most foster children carried their possessions. The second was battered, dirty and brown, as though it might have traveled a couple of times by slow boat around the Horn.

Mrs. Davis explained, "I give him that one. You don't need to bring it back. I got me some new bags last year."

Mrs. Davis was a large black woman who had been fostering children for over thirty years. A childless widow herself, she took her satisfaction in life from providing a safe haven for foster children. She was well liked and respected by all the childcare workers and her children all called her "Mom."

As Tracy carried the luggage to her trunk a small red head pushed its way around Mrs. Davis' skirt and declared, "You're not Sally. Where's Sally? Where's my caseworker?"

"Hi, Kelly. I'm Tracy. Don't you remember me? I'm the one who passed out the candy canes at the Christmas party. Miss Sally is sick with the flu. I get to go with you to Washington."

"Mom, I don't want her to take me. I want Sally. I'll just wait for Sally."

"Now, Kelly, you know you can't put off goin'. Your new family is expecting you this very day. Why, I'll bet they're already at that airport lookin' for you."

Kelly's freckled little face started to crumble as tears welled up and spilled over.

"Mom, I changed my mind. I don't want no new family. I just want to stay here with you. Tell her, Mom, tell her you're gonna keep me."

"Honey, you know that can't be. We been over this before. I'm just a 'Take Care Of Mom,' not a 'Keeping Mom.' Your new Mom in Washington is gonna be your Keeping Mom. I love you, Kelly, and I sure am gonna miss you, but you got to go now with Miss Tracy to get your very own family."

"Please, Mom, please don't let her take me."

By this time Maudie Davis had scooped Kelly up into her large embrace and was hugging him to her as she looked pleadingly over his shoulder at Tracy. Her tears fell like an anointing on his red curls. She set him down while bestowing a kiss of blessing on his forehead and another on his cheek.

"You go now with Miss Tracy. Remember to say your prayers. Jesus is gonna keep you safe."

Tracy choked back the enormous lump in her throat and struggled to hold back tears and force a smile as she reached for Kelly's hand. He released a sob but shrugged away her hand and wiped his nose on the sleeve of his shirt.

"I ain't no baby. I can walk by myself."

With unmistakable resolution, he straightened his forty-six inches and marched to the car ahead of her. He climbed into the front passenger seat and pulled the seat belt around him. He rolled down the window and turned to wave goodbye to Mrs. Davis. Tracy saw in her rearview mirror that Mrs. Davis was wiping away tears with both hands.

Tracy tried to make conversation during the twenty-minute drive to the airport. Kelly was not ready to accept her overtures. The life he knew, the world he knew, was ending. Tracy had reviewed his case file. She realized that Kelly likely had little memory of his life before being with Mrs. Davis. His birth mother was considered to be mildly mentally delayed. She had five children by three fathers before she was twenty-two. She was overwhelmed by the demands of parenting. One by one her children had been placed in foster care. Kelly came into the system at age two. He'd had three temporary foster homes before going to Mrs. Davis' at four years old. It was another two years before parental rights were severed and he became free for adoption. At six years old he fell into the category of "Special Needs" hard to place children.

That's when Sally Roberts was assigned his case. She had listed him in the national adoption register as well as the state posting of available children. At last, just after he turned eight in November, a family in Washington inquired about him. The family had been certified by the Washington adoption system but had not found there the child they sought. The couple, Michael and Sharon Fogarty, were in their early forties and had two high school age daughters. They made two trips to Arizona to meet Kelly and to let him get to know them. The first was a four-day visit. They did the round of child amusements, the zoo, McDonald's and such. They were satisfied that Kelly was the son they'd been hoping for. The second trip they brought their daughters. It was only for three days but the girls decided that Kelly was cuter than Snoopy and wanted to take him home with them right then. Of course, that had to wait on Judge Crawford's order, so now it was the end of January and he was finally on his way.

"Kelly, you will need to stay right beside me while we check in and while we wait to board the airplane. Do you understand that?"

Kelly was silent. Tracy glanced down at him. He looked very small and very forlorn. He was working his fingers back and forth on the seat belt. She noted his fingertips where the nails were chewed to the quick. This was a symptom of the uncertainties of his life that she observed to be in common with most of the children in the system.

"Will you do that, Kelly? Stay right beside me?"

He nodded but did not look up.

Tracy parked her car in the Park 'n Save lot. Kelly became apprehensive.

"What are we doin' here? This ain't the airport."

"It will just be for a few minutes and then we'll get on a shuttle bus that will take us there."

She had scarcely said the words when the shuttle pulled up beside them. The driver reached for Kelly's bags to load them aboard.

"Hey, those are mine! What you doin' with them?" Kelly grabbed the nearest bag and tried to wrest it out of the driver's hand. The man looked bewildered and wordlessly appealed to Tracy for help.

"It's okay, Kelly. He's just helping us get on the bus."

Kelly scowled but released his hold. "Aw right, I guess."

A three-minute ride brought them in front of the Alaska Airline drop off. This time Kelly let the driver unload their bags without protest. Tracy discovered that they were denied curbside check-in because of her status relative to Kelly. It would be necessary for them to check in at the main desk. She motioned to a Sky Cab assistant to carry the bags on a luggage dolly.

Kelly again was ready to do battle. "Where you goin' with my stuff? Them's mine!"

"Look. It's all right, Kid. I'm just helping your Mom take these inside."

"She ain't my Mom! Anyhow, I can help her get 'em in."

Tracy intervened. "Kelly, he's not going to steal our bags. He helps people with luggage all the time. That's his job."

Once inside they found a line at the reception desk. Kelly discovered the black belts that formed the lineup aisles were removable from their metal stands and proceeded to remove and realign them. Tracy's attention had been momentarily distracted until one of the attendants behind the counter called out, "M'am, please tell your son to leave the aisles in place."

Tracy turned around to find that Kelly was methodically closing each segment between the posts.

"Kelly, please put those back the way they were. They are there to help people get to the right desk."

He complied without further urging and turned his attention to examining the tags and other items on the reception counter. When Tracy lifted the bags through the luggage pass he again demanded to know where they were going. She patiently explained that they would be going on the same airplane in which they were about to travel but bags had to be loaded into the storage below where passengers sit. Although his look was skeptical, he accepted her explanation.

Boarding passes in hand, Tracy directed Kelly toward the concourse security station. Again she had to show I.D. and her authorization to be escorting Kelly. That went smoothly enough but when Kelly was directed to remove his jacket and shoes he exploded in fury.

"You can't take my shoes! Them's mine! Mom got them for me. You ain't gonna get my shoes!" With that declaration he jerked away from Tracy who had started to help him off with his jacket. He turned around and ran down the ramp toward the escalator that descended to the baggage claim area.

Tracy rolled her eyes and threw up her hands in total frustration. Charging after Kelly, she came close to tumbling down the escalator and in doing so nearly knocked over an old couple who were descending.

She called out, "Kelly, stop! Wait for me. They aren't going to keep your shoes. Let me explain."

Kelly had reached the baggage level and was confused about where to go next. He looked up at Tracy. His shoulders slumped and he burst into tears. Tracy caught up to him and knelt beside him. Taking a deep breath, she softly explained about the security measures that had recently been adopted. Of course Kelly had heard about the 9-11 disaster but he'd had no way of relating it to this, his first airplane trip. Once he understood he meekly followed her back up to the security checkpoint where the officers, who still held her handbag and papers, smiled in consternation.

After passing through the metal screening she was helping Kelly back into his jacket and felt bulky bulges in the pockets. She asked him to show her what he was carrying. He had purloined five baggage tags, two blue security instruction cards, two gum wrappers, a discarded ballpoint pen, and an empty Tic-Tac container. They still had thirty minutes left before boarding time. She offered to buy him a slice of pizza on condition that he dump his collection into a trash container. Her bribe worked.

With his pizza consumed, she asked him to go use the restroom and to be sure to wash his face and hands. Since she had neglected to tell him to dry them, they were wet and shining when he emerged. Their flight was being called so she pulled a tissue from the pack in her purse and hastily dabbed at his wet parts. He grimaced while trying to pull away from her. She reminded him of his agreement to stay right beside her.

The flight attendant checked their boarding passes and motioned them forward. Entering the long passageway Tracy felt a small moist hand slip into her own. Glancing down, she saw the face of a scared little boy determined to face all dangers.

Their seats were in advance of the wing. She gave Kelly the choice of the window seat or the middle seat. Predictably, he picked the window. She was glad that he'd have a clear view and hoped he would be entertained by that. Before she could stow her handbag and fasten her seat belt, Kelly had pulled out the airline magazines and barf bag, clicked loose his seat belt to punch the overhead light buttons, twisted full open the air cock, and summoned the flight attendant with the assistance light.

The flight attendant edged by the crowd of passengers still stowing carryons and asked, "How may I help you?"

With a sheepish look Tracy apologized, "I'm really sorry, Miss. This is his first flight and he was trying out the buttons. We don't need anything just now."

The attendant turned on a tolerant smile but the slight exasperation in her voice betrayed her annoyance. "Please try to see that he remains seated and buckled in for takeoff." To Kelly she said, "Young man, listen to your Mom. She wants to keep you safe."

Kelly shouted, "She ain't my Mom."

All the passengers in the first twelve rows turned to stare at them. Tracy wanted to sink beneath the seat. The flight attendant shook her head as she turned to begin shutting the overhead bays.

Tracy reiterated the admonition to fasten his seat belt. She pulled the loose end to bring it firmly around him. She was made again aware of how sleight he was. There was not much meat on him. A second person could have shared the belt with him and still have length left over. She foraged in her purse to find her pack of chewing gum and offered him a piece. He asked if he could have two so she handed him another. She didn't notice that he slipped the second into his pocket.

The intercom chimed and a man's voice announced, "This is your Captain speaking. Welcome aboard. We are in position for takeoff. Attendants secure the cabin and take your seats."

Tracy glanced at Kelly. To say he was "white knuckled" would have been understatement. His freckles made sharp contrast to the pallor of his face. He stared straight ahead as he felt the motion of the plane and the roar of the revving engines. The only thing she could see moving were his jaws as he chewed the gum to keep pace with the accelerating aircraft. He appeared to be holding his breath. As the plane lifted free of the tarmac he turned his head to the window and sucked in a great gulp of air.

"Hey, that's cool! I think I can see my house, I mean, my old house. And there's my old school." His grip on the armrest relaxed.

Tracy asked, "Were you scared when we started to take off?"

"Naw. It was fun. I guess the pilot knows how to fly this thing."

Soon after reaching cruising altitude the seat belt light was turned off and the attendants began beverage service. When the attendant asked, "What would you like to drink?" Kelly responded, "How much does it cost? I ain't got no money." She assured him it was a complimentary service at no charge.

"How about that? You mean I can have any of those and it don't cost nothing?"

She smiled and said, "It won't cost even a penny. Which one would you like?"

"You got Pepsi?"

"No, but I do have Coke or root beer?"

"Okay. I guess I'll have Coke."

She poured the cocktail glass full over ice and handed it to him.

"Hey, don't I get the whole can?"

"I suppose we can spare it," she said, grinning.

The attendant filled the remaining orders for their row and moved on. Kelly turned to Tracy and said, "That's a pretty good deal, ain't it, getting these for free?"

She said, "Yes, that's a pretty good deal."

Thirty minutes later Kelly whispered to her, "I gotta go. I don't think I can hold it 'til we get to Washington."

Tracy leaned down and whispered back, "You don't have to. There is a bathroom on the plane." She pointed to the door by the cockpit.

He immediately snapped free his seatbelt and climbed over her and their aisle seat partner. He ran to the restroom door and disappeared inside. The "Occupied" sign came on.

After five minutes lapsed Tracy began to be concerned. After ten minutes two passengers were waiting behind the First Class divider for a turn in the restroom. Tracy stopped the passing attendant and asked if she would knock on the door to check on Kelly. Kelly emerged at the knock, his face dripping water, and rubbing his wet hands down his shirt front.

"That place is really cool. The toilet doesn't fill up like the one at home. Where does the stuff go? Does it just dump out into the air? I sure wouldn't want to be down there and have it dump all over me."

Tracy said, "I think it goes into a holding tank that gets emptied when they service the airplane on the ground. What took you so long? Did you take a bath?"

"Naw. Mom made me take a bath last night, but I figured I ought to wash up before we get to Washington. Does everybody in Washington take a bath every day or do they just wash up?"

"I suppose they're just like folks in Arizona or anywhere. It's called 'Washington' because it's named for our first president, not because of their bathing habits."

The flight attendants had brought out the snack cart and were offering a sandwich this time. Kelly was again amazed that these too were for free. He dissembled the sandwich to examine its contents and removed the lettuce and tomato. Tracy directed him to wrap the rejected items in his napkin. He made quick work of the sandwich and happily anticipated a second can of soda when he realized the beverage cart was again being pushed down the aisle.

Setting a pattern, thirty minutes after the tray items were removed Kelly indicated he needed to use the bathroom again. Tracy sanctioned his need but sternly directed that he quickly wash only his hands and vacate the convenience so others could use it. Kelly nodded his understanding. This time he was in and out of the facility in about three minutes and wiping his wet hands down his damp shirt front.

"Why didn't you dry your hands on a paper towel?"

Kelly looked perplexed. "You said I should hurry and get right out."

He settled back into his seat and turned his attention to the window view. They were passing over heavily snow clad mountains shining in the sun. Kelly had only rarely seen snow on the mountain tops in Arizona.

"Hey, I bet if I was down there I could make the biggest snowman in the whole world."

Tracy smiled and said, "Yes, I bet you could."

He watched as they flew in and out of cloud banks with white drifts like great mounds of cotton candy. The sun was starting its decline and beginning to color the puffy blankets of clouds.

The Captain's voice came over the intercom to announce their approach to SeaTac airport and to remind them to remain seated with seatbelts secure until landed and parked at their terminal gate.

Kelly's obvious anxiety returned. He didn't have to be coached to pull his seatbelt tight. He gripped the armrests in each hand long before the plane began its landing descent.

"Tracy, do you think they'll really be there waiting for me? If they aren't you'll take me back to Mom's won't you?"

"Kelly, I'm sure they will be there to meet us. They swore to the judge that they will adopt you because they want you to be part of their family. They want you to be their son and be brother to their girls."

He protested, "But what if they changed their mind? What if they don't want me now? What if they ain't there when we get there? You'll take me back to Mom's won't you? Will you promise?"

Tracy could see he needed assurance that he wouldn't be abandoned. "I'm sure they'll be waiting for us but if, for any reason they aren't, I promise to keep you with me."

The plane was touching down now. It was a bumpy landing that caused Kelly to let go of the armrest between them and grab Tracy's arm. His grip was so tight she wondered if he might have drawn blood under her shirtsleeve. As the aircraft slowed he lessened his grasp. They began the taxiway to the proper concourse and Kelly unfastened his seatbelt. Tracy had to remind him of the Captain's instructions. He meekly complied.

He wasn't prepared for the aisle crush of people trying to retrieve carry on luggage when they finally parked at their gate. He wanted to rush off and push around people. Tracy had to restrain him. While they waited for their turn to exit Tracy used the opportunity to explain the procedure of claiming their bags and meeting the Fogartys by the baggage claim area. She tried to make it clear that only passengers are allowed beyond the security check where everybody has to take their shoes off.

In spite of her careful explanation, Kelly was scanning all the faces the minute they came out of the access corridor. It was a long walk from their point of deplaning to the baggage claim section. Although his legs were much the shortest, Tracy had to hustle to stay up with Kelly after he spotted the signs with arrows to Baggage. She tried to tell him they would have to wait a few minutes for the bags to get to the area from the airplane. At this point Kelly was much more intent on trying to find his new family than on the suitcases.

The crowd was dense with passengers from many flights milling to find the right carousel for their luggage. Tracy had no idea what the Fogartys looked like. She was scanning to spot a family group with two teenage girls. She scolded herself for not getting a better description before starting the trip. Of course, Kelly knew what to look for and they new Kelly so Tracy had to rely on their recognition. Just getting the right baggage conveyor was proving to be a challenge. Two displayed signs for Alaska Airline. Seeing other passengers from their flight prompted her decision between them. Looking about as they waited she could see no family likely to be the Fogartys. Kelly was becoming agitated.

"They ain't here. They ain't coming. They don't want me. Tracy we gotta go back. They said they'd be here but they ain't!"

Tracy was simultaneously pulling their bags off the conveyor and grasping Kelly's shoulder to keep him from bolting. "Kelly, I'm sure they are here somewhere. You can't see them for the crowd. Help me with these suitcases." She jammed his new bag into his hand. It served to stop him for the moment. However, as the crowd around the carousel began to thin out Tracy, too, began to worry.

She suggested, "Let's go over to the next one. They must be waiting there."

Kelly struggled with his burden and Tracy carried her own bag and his old one. She was thinking they must look like a couple of refugees as they made their way. To their disappointment, the crowd was thinning by the second round-about as well, and there was no sign of the family. Kelly's lower lip was trembling and tears were welling. Tracy felt her mouth go dry and a lump form in her throat. She thought, I can't break down now. This child needs all the support I can muster. I can't believe those people would flake out on a little kid. They've got to be here somewhere.

Noise was increasing in the area as new planes discharging passengers released a flow of humanity. A loudspeaker offered a disembodied voice saying, "Will passenger Kelly Malone please come to the Baggage Claim office. Your party is waiting for you."

Tracy and Kelly squealed together, "That's us! They're here!"

Spotting the office where unclaimed luggage is stored, they grabbed their bags and ran. Waiting by the glass door was the unmistakable family. They ran forward to embrace Kelly in a group hug. Tracy stood aside in wonder. Her tears finally spilled over, but now they were of joy. All four Fogartys looked up at her and grinned. Their bright red hair and freckled faces were a perfect match to the small boy in their midst. For his part, Kelly would have taken a prize for *Standing Broad Grin*, it spread from ear to ear. Michael and Sharon stood up. "You must be Tracy. We can't thank you enough for bringing our Kelly safely to us. When we couldn't find him in the crowd we got really worried that something bad had happened. It was so confusing. We didn't quite know where to wait for you. You must be tired from the trip. Will you join us for dinner? We need to eat before we go home. It's a long drive from here to Puyallup, that's actually where we live."

Tracy was tempted but instead she said, "Thanks, no. It has been a long day. I'd like to just check in to my hotel. It's just across the way from the terminal. This is your time and Kelly's to celebrate his new family.

Kelly, I guess it's time to say 'goodbye,' would it be okay if I give you a hug?"

Kelly's new sisters stepped back and let him move out of their little circle. He edged forward while examining his shoes and allowed Tracy to embrace him. He murmured into her ear, "Thanks for the pizza and gum, and for bringing me here."

She whispered back, "It was my pleasure. Have a happy life."

As they collected his bags and turned to leave, Kelly looked back and gave her a little wave. Tracy couldn't swallow the great lump in her throat.

Tracy left the terminal humming *Has Anybody Here Seen Kelly?*

Mary

NEIGHBOR

A man who lives next door
Seldom goes out
And almost never leaves the house,
Because, you see,
He doesn't want
To be disturbed;
He reads a lot
And writes his memoirs by heart . . .

Besides, he says,
The house has many rooms,
Each one with memories its own,
And when he wants,
He goes from room to room
To hear their stories from the past,
The ones that happened
Long ago . . .

Lana

A BOTTLE OF GRIEF

Oh, I know everyone falls in love with his therapist, but I want you to know . . . I am NOT in love with her.

I didn't even want to go see a shrink, but the Captain said it is POLICY. Whenever an officer is involved in a shooting, it is policy to have a therapist conduct a Critical Incident Debriefing. He made it a big deal, pronouncing the capital letters! If I refused to go, I could be suspended for lack of cooperation. Everyone knows that I'm a bad-ass cop who can handle ten shootings, but I sure didn't want to lose my badge. I'd play their stupid game, tell her what she wants to hear and get out of there.

The expected 'And how do you feel about that?' never came. She asked why I had come to see her, so I told her. The Captain made me. I thought she was going to ask me about the shooting, but she didn't. She said to tell her about me. I'll play it her way, I thought, and gave her my canned spiel: both parents deceased, married, two children, love my job. I thought that would be enough, but she asked about my wife, the two boys. She didn't ask anything about the job. Although that seemed to be the purpose of this farce, I played it her way, just to get it over with.

She listened. I don't mean that her ears heard my words. They did, but I could tell by the expressions that passed over her face, she was really listening to me. I felt like she was hearing more than I said. No one has ever done that before. My wife loves me and listens to my words, but she doesn't hear what I'm not saying. And the boys, well, teenage boys only hear the roaring of their own hormones.

Before I knew it, time was up and she was telling me she would like me to come back. Since it hadn't been as bad as I thought it would be, I agreed. After all, the department is paying for it and my time.

The next time, she started by repeating something I had said last time and asked about it. Something about being a dad. I had forgotten saying it, and she remembered without even looking at my file. She said it made her curious about what my father was like. Her voice was so quiet and casual. I thought therapists dug and probed. I felt her tone and the incredibly expressive "listening" face were leading me by the hand to a safe place.

I told her about growing up in Toledo and my dad being gone a lot. He was a manufacturer's representative, whatever that is, I never knew. She asked me what kind of a father he was, and it was like she'd pulled a cork out of a bottle!

"He was a mean alcoholic who got meaner the more he drank. Something always got broken when he came home. He'd either fall into or onto it, or he would sweep it off the table, like it was there just to piss him off. He'd hit and maybe ask questions later. He wouldn't stop hitting until my mom tried to stop him. Then he'd turn on her. She usually had a shiner, either black or just changing colors. She was missing two teeth and had a scar on her lip from him throwing a bottle at her. He would finally pass out, get up the next day and leave for work as if nothing had happened."

"Did you have siblings?" Her voice was soft, like gentle hands bandaging a wound. It got to me. I had been replaying those old tapes in my mind like I was still there, hearing my old man's voice and smelling his boozy stink. I instantly saw my older brother finally standing up to the abuse.

"That man beat my brother so bad that he fell to the floor and passed out. After several kicks, the old man passed out too." Tears I hadn't shed for thirty years came pouring out.

"I helped my mom carry my brother to his bed and we sat with him all night. When he didn't come to by morning, she called for help. My brother died that day from a ruptured liver. He bled to death internally."

"And then . . . ?"

"My dad was arrested and sent to prison. He was to get out in 3 years and 2 months, but he was stabbed by another inmate. He deserved to die, but killing was too good for him, too easy."

"Your mom . . . ?"

"She died before he did, of shame and a broken heart."

Why couldn't she have just asked me about the shooting? I felt things I hadn't felt since the day my brother died . . . pain I never wanted to feel again, rage so powerful it was a searing agony, a grief so deep I could fall into it. And yet . . . And yet there was a part of my soul that felt washed clean, unloaded, light.

I almost hate her for making me feel those things. No, I don't love her. But maybe, just maybe, there will be another shooting I'll need to see her about.

JoLynne

GRANDMA ESS

Grim. Rigid. Fearsome In all the cobwebbed halls of memory, this image of Grandma Ess never changes. The same acid-sour nausea threatens to rise in my throat as I remember how my 7 year old eyes saw her.

Thin, white hair in a scalping-tight braid is wound around her head. White bobbie-pins wouldn't dare let even one strand loose. As thin and straight as the pillar next to her, she seems to be all one washed-out color with pale skin and faded calico apron.

I wonder how she knows exactly when we will arrive. She is always waiting on the front porch, even though she never seems happy to see us. As usual, her greeting is sharp.

"Well, it's about time you got here. I was ready to give up on you."

I don't expect any smiles or hugs from her any more. Some grandmas have them and some don't. She doesn't have any at all. I try to give her some of mine, but she doesn't seem to notice she needs them. Maybe they are just too much bother.

For someone so sour, Grandma Ess makes the best cookies in the world. They are two layers of crispy sugar cookies with homemade mincemeat sandwiched between. The top layer has a moon face cut into it. We'd better not ask for any! She doesn't believe it is polite for children to ask for anything, but should wait until it is offered. Of course, no cookies will be offered unless Judy has grown the most.

Judy is my half-sister who lives with Grandma Ess. Her mother died when Judy was a 9-week-old infant, and Grandma Ess brought her here to the old farmhouse to live. She is two years older than I am, and everybody tells us we look alike.

Oh, no! This is the part I always hate! It makes my stomach feel squeezy! We have to stand in the hot sun on the front sidewalk until Judy comes out. She always hides when we come to visit because she doesn't like this part either.

Grandma Ess grabs me by one elbow, and swings me around to stand back-to-back with Judy. With one sharp, bony finger in the middle of my chest she pushes me, hard, until I bump into Judy's back.

"Now, stand up straight, both of you. Let's see who has grown the most," she demands in her high-pitched whine.

Boy, I hate this! I know I've grown the most this time, because Mom was complaining my jeans are too short again. Maybe, if I scrunch down, just a little.

"I said stand up straight!" Her voice hurts like a toothache, and so does the poke in the ribs with that bony finger.

Maybe Judy will get up on her tiptoes, and maybe, just maybe, Grandma Ess won't notice!

"Girls, I want you two to quit fooling around and stand up straight! Humph." She puts so much meanness into a "Humph!"

"I see that Jo is the tallest this time," she nearly hisses. "Well, what are you standing around for? Come on in the house. We're letting in the heat with the door standing open." Her voice is as piercing as the screech of the screen door spring.

That settles that! The grownups go in, shutting out the heat and flies. We straggle to the backyard. We've failed again! Neither of us is in the mood to play now. We know from experience Grandma Ess is going to be grumpy the rest of the visit. There won't be any "Man in the Moon" cookies this time!

We complain about being too hot to play, but we aren't fooling each other. As we slump on the swings, idly scuffing our shoes in the dust, we are both thinking the same thing.

"This is sure going to be a long visit. Who cares who is the tallest? I try to grow the way she wants me to, but I never do it right. Why can't she like us just the way we are? We'd like to like her, . . . if she'd let us."

JoLynne

WOMAN SOLDIER

Woman-soldier walked on the battle field,
When the field had fallen still.
She had a Red Cross on her left sleeve
And a bag across her shoulder.

Her blue-eagle eyes searched for wounded,
Among the bodies of slaughtered soldiers,
The soldiers without uniforms, old disabled men and women,
Along with young boys and girls,
Who fought the German Army with bare hands!

Woman-soldier walked and walked for hours . . .
Then stopped and knelt
Her strong shoulders sank; her dilapidated bag slipped down,
Her blue eyes . . . red now, filled with tears.

She frowned at Heaven, begging for answers
She had not found many wounded alive, who could use her help
While her tears were falling on WARSAW ground,
Covered with blood and the dead.

Tatiana

WAITING PRACTICE

What a dinky waiting room. No wonder there are so many people sitting out in the vestibule and hallway. I guess I should have called ahead but she said it will just be a few minutes. I should count myself lucky that I have a place to sit, cramped as it is—what a sorry assortment of magazines. I haven't needed to read *Parenting* in the last thirty years, anyway, it's *something*.

Children are eating junk food daily and gaining over ten pounds a year in excess body weight. That's supposed to be news? Who's going to eat all those billions of Big Macs if the kids don't? I wonder if I'm supposed to fast before I go to the Cancer Center. All they told me was to collect the MRI pictures and the other reports and x-rays.

Thank goodness the MRI is behind me. That's an ordeal I hope I won't have to repeat. "About 45 minutes . . ." Yeah, right. That was just the warm up. I thought my arm was going to be permanently paralyzed before it was over. I didn't help that I had to wait fifteen empty minutes for the doc to come in and take his turn at poking a needle in my vein for the dye. At least my bruises match—one on each hand. God's grace didn't abandon me. I felt like I was closed in my coffin in that claustrophobic chamber but singing hymns in my mind worked as good as hypnotism. I honestly didn't realize I was in there a whole hour and a half.

What's this tiny baby doing here? The mom looks really worried.

"How old is your baby?"

"He's two weeks old. He's not well."

I don't think she wants to talk. She's probably too scared. Am I scared? Yes, damn it. I don't want to be. I don't like the feeling. I don't like heights; I don't like roller coasters; I don't like tight places, and I don't like feeling scared. I never understood those people who paid good money to see horror movies.

Why in the world did the doctor order a chest x-ray? The problem is in my arm, not my chest. And all that blood work—is he prepping me for surgery? He did say they will likely do a biopsy when I go to the Cancer Center. Maybe I should be glad that he didn't *practice* his medicine on me when he admitted that he doesn't know what to make of the *thing*.

"Hello, Mary. How are you?"

Who is this man? He looks familiar but I can't place him. Obviously he thinks he knows me and he does know my name.

"Hello. Nice to see you. I'm here waiting for pictures. I plan to autograph them and send them to all my friends. They told me they got some good ones." What a stupid dumb thing to say. I should know him—he must have been a former client.

"Well, it looks like we may have a long wait."

We've exhausted that subject. What next?

Who's this pushy broad forcing her way to the window?

"Miss—Miss, how much longer will I have to wait? I've been here over an hour and I have another appointment to keep."

"I'm very sorry Mrs. Warner, but the doctor is backed up. He shouldn't be much longer."

"Well, I'm not waiting any longer."

Good. She's been throwing out dirty looks since I got here. Good riddance. I feel like I'm *Waiting for Godot*. There's something slightly surreal about this. Ralph Waite was in the television production I saw of the play. He seemed a most unlikely actor for such a serious classic existential play. Perhaps he was chosen for his name. As I recall he was very good in it.

"Ms Alexander—your pictures are ready."

My goodness! They're huge, much bigger than regular x-rays.

"Thank you very much." At last I'm out of here. I still don't remember the man's name.

There's a printed report in the envelope. What's it say? "liposarcoma, . . . synovial carcoma, . . . malignant fibrous histiocytoma, . . . *MOST LIKELY TO REPRESENT A MALIGNANT SOFT TISSUE TUMOR.*

I've never liked horror movies.

Mary

T. A. D.

My parents came to an agreement. Pa would name the boys and Ma would name the girls. Ma tended toward the Biblical with Ruth, Naomi and Esther. She liked the name Dinah, but thought Dinah Dunning sounded like a burlesque queen. She was afraid Pa would name us boys like the German families in the area did, after every uncle and grandfather, living or dead. Those poor boys ended up with initials that were a sentence in themselves. Fortunately Pa, being a reading man, favored inventors so their two were Thomas Alva and Alexander Graham Dunning.

I liked my name, not only because Pa admired Mr. Edison, but because my initials made a word. My brother hated his, not because of Mr. Bell, but because of the nasty way kids would stretch out Alexander, making it whiny and mocking.

When he grew up and went into business, he used A. Graham Dunning, said it sounded more prosperous. Me, I stuck with what I had. My workmates called me Tad, and close friends called me Tom. Either way, I knew when it was dinnertime.

Growing up on a farm educated me in ways to fix things, make do or do without. Both of my parents could read and write. Beyond that, they were mostly self-taught. Ma read Godey's Ladies Book, enjoying the serial stories continued each month. Pa stumbled onto a set of Classics at an estate sale and read them until the covers were worn thin. He probably knew all the stories by heart just from reading them so often, sometimes out loud to the family.

Instead of pushing us to read his classics, he'd get us interested in an exciting part of a story, then bet us we couldn't tell him how the story ended. These bets began to include memorizing important speeches, and of course, he always expressed regret at losing the bet. My memory is not so good these days, but every once in a while, Caesar's address to Brutus, or some verses of Hiawatha come back to me.

Ma sold the farm when Pa died and moved to town where she could do dressmaking and help the girls with their little ones. I got a job in a woolen mill, but had an itch to get back outdoors so quit and worked for a horse trader who was gathering up stock for the Army. Things were heating up over in Europe and war talk became more common.

One of my duties was to break the untamed horses. It wasn't my favorite thing to do, but it saved me from going to the trenches. One of those pesky horses threw me, then stepped on my leg. It put me out of the horse business and out of the line-up for the Army. By the time I healed enough to work, there was a shortage of men for local jobs, so I got a job as a guard at the prison farm. I only had to be able to sit on a horse and shoot a shotgun to qualify as one of the guards over the road crew. I didn't much like seeing those fellows in leg irons, but some of them were real bad actors. None ever gave me any trouble, which I am thankful for.

Having a decent steady wage made me think about settling down. Charlotte, the helper at the boarding house where I stayed, caught my eye. She was a pretty little thing, not too flighty and didn't seem to be afraid of work. She didn't mind my gimpy leg and was pleased about my dream to buy some land to start apple orchards. We were married in the fall, lived in a little house not far from the prison farm and saved every spare nickel for our orchard. She didn't seem to mind me bringing one of my buddies from work home for a meal once in a while. Because our shifts changed, she got to know most of the guys.

I guess she got to know them a little too well. One payday, I went home from night shift just at first daylight. Charlotte and one of the men from the other shift were sound asleep in our bed. Neither one of them roused as I gathered up my clothes and left. I never looked back.

Wandering down the Pacific coast, taking odd jobs here and there, I finally got past that gut-stabbing pain. If Ma taught us anything, it was that life goes on. What you think is going to kill you doesn't, and then you have to keep living.

After stints as a dishwasher, a bartender and a short-order cook, I was offered a job as cook on a shrimp boat. My gimpy leg helped me learn to balance myself on that rolling boat. Cooking on a stove that swings with the rolls made any other job easy. I liked the hours of solitude and being at the mercy of the weather. This lasted seventeen seasons, until a big storm tore us up too much and we limped back to port, with only a partial catch.

The cold and damp hadn't been good for my leg, so I decided it was time to try a landlocked job. I drifted up to Idaho and then over to Montana. The Basque sheepherders came into the bar I tended and were friendly to me. When I said I missed being outdoors, they laughingly invited me to learn to herd sheep. I took them up on it. I wound up driving one of those little hump-backed sheepherders' wagons, with a black and white dog and two mules for company, up to the high meadows of Montana. In the fall, after taking the sheep down the mountain, I worked as a cook in the shearing camp until it was time to go upcountry again. I lost track of how many years I put in doing that. It was a good life, since I didn't need much in the way of entertainment. It's a fine way for a man to get to know himself and notice his world

One winter, I met a fellow who was hauling crude out of the oil fields. We just seemed to hit it off. He was kind of like the son I didn't have. Not only could he keep up with me in swapping stories, he was a worthy opponent at cribbage. We passed a good many snowy nights this way.

I had a nasty bout of pneumonia and this friend took me home to his family until I recovered. As much as I enjoyed my solitary life, I learned that I could take family living. I was unofficially adopted, becoming Grandpa to a boy and girl who were glad to learn to play cribbage and didn't mind my stories.

When I was healthy again, I was lucky enough to get a job in the little town only a few miles away from my new family. The small hotel needed a desk clerk, bartender and cook. The owner was glad to get someone who could do it all. The job suited me. The hotel and I just wore out together.

It's been a long life full of experiences and good people. I have few regrets. They are a waste of time. I've seen and done lots of things most people never get the chance to see or do.

When you get around to making the marker, just put T.A.D., November 17, 1898 and my last date. I know who I am . . . and I'm content.

JoLynne

TO MY FRIEND

I wouldn't be surprised
If men start following you around
Staring hard at your decolletage,
No, I wouldn't be surprised . . .

You are petite, brunette,
With curves galore,
And if you didn't realize it yet,
That's what all men are looking for . . .

And further more,
When you are walking
Down the isle at your
Favorite grocery store,

I wouldn't blink an eye
If men would stand in line
To get a closer look
At your revealing decoltage,

That comes without a hint
Of even slightest camouflage . . .

Lana

ONE OF US

No one remembers when Camie Lewis came to our small town. She just seemed to be there always, in the little shack by the railroad tracks. She lived alone and didn't visit or even talk to the neighbors. She took care of her chickens and the old cat that came around, dug in her garden and minded her own business.

Camie was just *different*. She seemed to me to be tall and skinny. She usually wore bib overalls and a man's faded flannel shirt, with scuffed work boots, not like a girl at all. Her mousy hair looked like it had been hacked off with pruning shears. She looked old and never seemed to change. Her beaky nose had a mole near the tip and made us kids whisper about her being a witch.

And she was the target of our pranks. Some of the boys tried the *burning paper bag of fresh manure on the doorstep* trick a second time, and found the tables had turned. She was waiting for them and doused them with a full bucket of water. Her creaky front gate had warned her they were up to no good. No one else ever went to her door.

Every Halloween, high school boys stole the outhouse out of her back garden and put it on the front steps of the school building. Camie must have heard their whispers and swearing about the smell, but she never stopped them. The constable and the principal always made the same boys put back the one-holer the next day. At the principal's insistence, they had to face her. When they stammered, "We're sorry, ma'm," she just nodded. It shamed them, but not enough to keep them from doing it the next year.

Every month Camie pulled a little red wagon across the highway to downtown four blocks away. She started at the Post Office for her one piece of mail. Then she went to the bank to cash a small check. After that she went to our only grocery store to pick up stuff. Coffee, lard, flour, cornmeal and sugar were about all she ever bought. The rest she grew in her own yard. Once in a while she stopped at the Co-op for kerosene, lamp oil and seeds for her garden.

Blooming vines covered the weathered wood of her ramshackle house. Everybody said her garden was the best in town, with its rows of corn, beans, hills of potatoes, squash, peas and greens. Her apple and cherry trees were tempting, but none of us ever dared go into her yard to steal fruit. Kids really liked her fancy hollyhocks that grew along the fence though, and stole the buds and blossoms for hollyhock dolls.

Not many of us ever heard Camie talk. When she was greeted, she just nodded. She only spoke when she had to, and didn't look anyone in the eye. Of course everyone talked about her because she was different, but her neighbors would have liked her if she had given them a chance.

Our town was finally able to do something for her. On one of her trips to town, a fast car hit her as she crossed the highway. Her little red wagon was smashed flat and Camie never knew it. The whole town went to her funeral. She was buried in her overalls, the only clothes she had. The volunteers of the Fire Department carried her coffin. One of them said, "Of course, we would do this. Camie was one of us, even if she didn't know it."

Months later a man in a fancy suit, driving a fancy car, came to town. He seemed to have business at the bank. Pretty soon, Russell Bowdeman, the druggist and mayor, and Casey Dodge from the Ford garage, hurried to the bank. After a while, all three of them were shaking hands with Mr. Green, the banker, in front of the bank. Within an hour, the whole town was buzzing about the new library we were going to have, the Camilla Winston Lewis Library.

I guess she did know she was one of us.

JoLynne

DISTRESSED

Distressed, she walked quickly out the facility's automatic doors.
Wondering, what now? What should she do now?
How can she cope with the numerous problems she's
Confronted with and how could she know if she
would be making the best decisions for her Mother?
Oh, Mom, she thought, how did all this happen to us,
Especially since Dad just died less than a year ago,
And Bobby left home, joined the Marines, and now is overseas.

Mother, no longer the person she once was,
Sat besides her in the recreation room where others stood or wandered,
Her Mom stared at her trying to focus with a drooping right eyelid,
Then asked her who was she, and what was she doing there?
Unable to lift her right arm, she moved her hand slightly from side to side.
"Look at my k-kitty," she said, "her-her f-f-fur s-s-s-o soft and p-p-pretty."
"I'm Laura, your daughter," the woman next to her said.
"I l-l-l-love k-k-kitty" the mother said, as she continued to pet her kitty.

It wasn't that long ago they had spent hours together
Talking, listening to music, watching favorite TV shows, enjoying each other
Sometimes arguing about one thing or another,
then laughing and being silly,
Or working and cooking up their favorite meals, and gathering and fixing
Whatever they could concoct, sharing their "specialties" with others.
Those were the fun days, the better days, never to be forgotten
And it seems like only yesterday that they happened.
Now Mother does not even recognize her daughter. How sad.

Laura, holds back tears, has mixed emotions and is overwhelmed,
Walking slowly towards her car after kissing her Mom, not wanting to leave
But knows she must, tears now streaming down her cheeks.
She makes no attempt to dry her face,
She loves her Mother dearly, but feels so helpless,
Trying to comprehend what life is all about, trying to live with some inevitables
With time, will she accept that her Mom had a stroke and has Alzheimer's?
How do I deal with this now she wondered, and looked up to the sky.

Loretta

SHOWDOWN
AT THE METEETSE HOTEL

Red hauled his husky, middle-aged frame out of the cab of the crude oil-tanker, being careful to avoid the patch of ice on the running board. Thumpety-bumping down those steps once already this week made every fiber of his six-foot body ache. The fatigue of fighting snowdrifts and the constant Wyoming wind added to the slouching slide that carried him through the snowy dusk into the small hotel. His sidekick, the black and white border collie named Fella, was his usual small shadow at Red's heels. Hauling crude out of the Big Horn Basin oil fields was a helluva way to earn a living, particularly in the middle of a blizzard.

Right now, the prospect of coffee-laced bourbon, a big bowl of Ol' Tom's belly-scalding chili, and a few relaxing games of cribbage with the aged night clerk/cook/bottle washer kept Red's dragging feet moving. It was a good thing the elk antler coat rack on the wall was on his way to the big round oak table in the middle of the room. If he had needed to take any extra steps to hang up his sheepskin jacket and Stetson, none of them would have made it to their destination. Fella was already stretched out on the rag rug under the table.

As Red's booted feet hit the scarred hardwood floor, three pairs of eyes turned his way. Two cowboys from the big ranch down the road leaned against the pint-sized bar, which also served as a front desk. They gave him a wide-eyed stare, and then greeted him with, "Man, did you drive through that howler? Don't you know the highway is closed until morning? The Smokies won't even let us go the few miles back to the Pitchfork Ranch tonight."

Red seemed too tired to do more than growl in reply. As he sank into the sturdy chair at the table, he rumbled, "Gimme the usual, Tom."

The little man behind the bar grunted back at him, then wiped his hands on the apron that swaddled his round belly. The rolling gait of his bandy legs was a leftover of his days as a shrimp boat cook. Now, those stubby legs brought him back with a bowl heaped high with meat and beans, and a pint of coffee and bourbon. He slid them in front of Red and gave Fella a meaty steak bone. The cowboys turned back to their drinks and conversation with matched shrugs. Red silently worked his way through the steaming chili and coffee, while Fella gnawed away at his steak bone.

At last the spoon clattered into an empty bowl, and Red set down the equally empty mug.

"Okay, old man, bring out your board and cards. I'm gonna wallop you tonight." Fella looked up with a "woof," temporarily abandoning the steak bone.

"You just think you are," cackled the old man, his Kewpie-doll tuft of hair waving in defiance. He sat down across from Red at the big table and began dealing the cards, six to each of them. Both placed their two cards in the crib and Red turned up the hold card.

"Ha," huffed Ol' Tom in satisfaction as he pegged his first score.

The only words spoken after that counted the points in the mysterious way of cribbage players, "Fifteen-two, fifteen-four, and a double run of three for eight is twelve!" The old man's topknot bobbed as he chortled at his long lead. The pegs in the other column on the board had barely crept ahead for the count of two pair. This continued as the pegs rounded the board a second time, and Tom's pegs crossed the finish line. At the end of the sixth game, Tom was fairly bouncing in his chair from the excitement of pegging that many winning games in a row. Red remained silent, but looked more grim with each loss. Fella tired of the one-sided contest and decided a nap under the table was more interesting.

As Tom's pegs marked the seventh win, Red rose and slapped his cards on the table with a loud thwack. Fella roused from his snooze with his ears pointed straight up. He sat up with a muttered growl, fixing an unblinking stare on Tom. Without a word, Red turned and went out into the snow without slowing for hat, coat, or dog. Ol' Tom tilted his chair away from Fella, but chuckled to himself.

The two cowboys had begun to watch the game out of boredom, and their eyes widened at the force of the slap of the cards on the table. They stared in puzzlement and surprise as Red went out the door.

Before Tom's chuckle could die away, Red was back, carrying a huge Colt .45 revolver. He ignored the eyes that followed him across the floor, as well as the snow melting on his hair and shoulders. He strode to the table with more energy than he had shown all evening, and with careful precision laid the gun on the table near his right hand.

"Now, let's not have any more cheating!"

The cowboys' eyes goggled, and they faded back, wordlessly scuttling up the stairs out of shooting range. One of them muttered something about someone being crazy. As the door of their room closed carefully, Tom and Red leaned back in their chairs, roaring with laughter. Aches, pains and snowstorms were forgotten. Fella joined in with an excited "Yip!" of his own.

Tom slapped the table with his hand. "That was even better than the last time we pulled it! Did you see their faces? Those boys had eyes like silver dollars! That was a good one, hunh, Fella? I can't wait until our next blizzard!"

Mopping his eyes and still chuckling, Tom went to pour them each another bourbon while Red shuffled the cards.

Funny thing, Ol' Tom didn't win another game all night!

JoLynne

GOODBYE, JAKE

The day began like any other school day, but when I got home I found out that things would never be the same again.

Jake's my brother. He took me with him to watch his soccer practice and sometimes he got me ice cream on the way home. I liked watching him playing his Game Boy. He was really good.

I was in my class, the second grade, when my teacher, Mrs. Bell, told me that my Aunt Beth was there to take me home. I wondered why I was leaving school so early and why my mom wasn't picking me up. The school counselor walked me to the office to meet Aunt Beth.

"Where's Mom? Aunt Beth, how come you're here?"

She had a weird look on her face and her eyes were red. She said, "Daniel, your mom asked me to pick you up."

All the way home she was sniffling and wiping her eyes. My Aunt Beth always laughs a lot, but that day she was acting strange.

"Why didn't Mom pick me up?" I asked her again. "Is she okay?" There was a tight feeling in my belly.

"Your mom's fine, Daniel, she's just upset."

"What's she upset about? Did Jake run away again?" I didn't remember him going to school that morning.

Aunt Beth blew her nose and said, "Your mom and dad need to tell you what's happening. We'll be home in a moment."

When we got to my house a whole bunch of people were there. Grandma and Grandpa, Uncle Charley, Sue and Bill who live next door, and some other people I don't know. Everybody was sort of whispering. I didn't see Mom or Dad but I could hear noises from upstairs like somebody crying. Aunt Beth took me into the kitchen and told me to wait there until she came back. She gave me a glass of milk and two cookies.

Pretty soon she came back and said, "Come upstairs quietly, Daniel. Your mom and dad need to talk to you now."

"Where's Jake?" Something's wrong, I thought, and suddenly I felt afraid.

"Just wait. They will tell you."

Mom was sitting on the bed and Dad was in a chair beside her. She was wiping tears off her face and Dad was blowing his nose in a big white handkerchief. She patted the bed for me to sit beside her.

Dad said, "Daniel, your mother and I have some very sad news about Jake."

"Did he get in an accident?" I asked.

"No. It wasn't an accident. Jake took his own life. He killed himself. It's called 'suicide.'"

What Dad was saying didn't sound real. "But he'll be all right, won't he? Is he in the hospital?"

Mom made a funny choking noise and started crying real loud. Dad reached over to hug her and then he turned to me and said, "Daniel, I'm telling you Jake won't be all right. He's dead. He won't be coming home ever again. They took him away to get him ready for his funeral. You will be able to say goodbye to him at the funeral."

Aunt Beth took my hand and pulled me toward the door. She was crying again, too.

I wanted to get away all by myself. I started to go to the basement, but Aunt Beth yanked me back. "Daniel, stay away from there! You can't go down to the basement today!"

I couldn't understand why she sounded so mad or why she wouldn't let me go down there. I turned around and went outside and sat on the back porch steps. Our dog Rusty came over and licked my hand.

I've seen funerals on television. There would be a big long box and people would stand around it and cry. I was thinking about how it would be if Jake never came home again and it made me cry. Rusty put his paws on my knees and his big old tongue licked at my tears.

It got dark pretty soon and Grandpa called me in to supper. I didn't feel like eating, but Grandma said I should at least eat my potatoes and gravy. Then they let me go upstairs to my bedroom.

The funeral was on Friday. Aunt Beth helped me get dressed in my Sunday School clothes.

"Please try to sit quietly in church, Daniel," she said. "It will be all right if you cry. Everybody is sad about Jake dying, so lots of people will

be crying. Do you want to go up to see him one last time and tell him goodbye?"

"I don't know, Aunt Beth. I think so, but I'm scared."

"Don't be afraid, Grandpa will be with you."

"But in the Harry Potter movies, dead people are scary."

Aunt Beth gave me a sad smile. "His body will look like he's asleep. His spirit is already in heaven."

The church was full. All our relatives were there, also Jake's school friends and lots of people. Some of them I didn't know, but they knew Mom and Dad.

The church music was slow, not the kind Jake liked to hear. There were lots of flowers. I wondered if Jake liked those. I went with Grandma and Grandpa up in front to see him. I had to stand on tiptoe to look in the box. They called it a casket. He looked like he was asleep. He was in his Sunday School clothes, but his shirt collar seemed to be pushing against his chin, with his tie too tight. I tried to reach in to fix it but Grandpa pulled my hand back. Grandma and Grandpa were praying while we stood there. All I said was, "Goodbye, Jake, I love you. I wish you didn't die."

After church was over everybody followed the black car that carried the casket and we all went to the cemetery, where they buried him. Then we went home. Mom and Aunt Beth passed around sandwiches and little cookies. People hugged Mom and Dad and said how sorry they were. I sat in a corner and thought about Jake. I heard two people I didn't know whispering. One said, "Why would a bright young kid like that want to go and hang himself?" The other said, "It's hard to figure teenagers these days."

I thought about that for a while, and then I remembered Aunt Beth stopping me from going downstairs. It must have been because that's where Jake died. I remembered that person saying he hanged himself. I wondered where he found out how to do that? Was it on T.V.?

Now our house seems so quiet and sad. Mom and Dad don't laugh much anymore. I wish I could hear the sound of Jake's music and the toots, tones, rings, and whistles from his GameBoy. I miss his friends, with their jokes and crazy games. Sometimes when I come home from school I think I'll see Jake and his friends playing basketball in the driveway. Then I remember that Jake is gone and it makes me cry.

Alone in my room I wonder why Jake killed himself. Did I do something to make him sad? Did he know how much he'd hurt me, Mom and Dad, his friends, and all the people who cared about him? The more I think about that, the madder I get. But those angry feelings make me feel guilty. How can I be mad at him? I hate feeling so mixed up.

Dad said, "It wasn't your fault, Daniel. It was Jake who was mixed up and didn't like himself. You were a good brother. I just wish he had talked to us about how he felt."

Maybe someday I'll be able to understand why I had to say, "Goodbye, Jake."

Mary

THE BOY NAMED BILLY

"Hi, Mama!" a voice shouted as I opened the gate. I turned and looked around. In front of the door stood a tall boy grinning from ear to ear. He had dark brown hair, a short crew cut, and a twinkle in his eyes. His clothes were wrinkled, shirt partially buttoned, with a pair of unzipped khaki shorts, and was barefoot.

"Hi!" I quickly replied as he turned and ran away from me. As quickly as he ran off, he returned extending he arm reaching out to touch me. Not expecting the gesture, I automatically drew back.

"Haa, mama scare," he said laughingly and ran off. Suddenly, he stopped. He did a quick movement of his right foot, then ran off again.

"Laura, look out!" called Renee as she pushed me to the side as a little something whizzed by me. Renee, my supervisor, had worked at this institution on Oahu for a couple years and was orienting me to the facility.

"Whew, glad it missed," she said.

"What was that?" I asked.

"Oh, just a piece of somebody's stool that didn't get picked up right away. Billy's learned to toss things like that from the floor with a flick of his toes and thinks it's funny," she said. Billy's now sixteen years old. He's been here since he was eight. He was born normal, the youngest of four and the only son. Unfortunately, when he was about 6 years old, he became very ill. He suffered from a number of seizures before they could get help. His illness caused permanent brain damage resulting in erratic and inappropriate behaviors. Now, he rarely has seizures, but does have behavior problems." Renee paused then continued as we to walked around the room.

"His dad couldn't handle the situation and deserted the family after about a year. His mom tried her best to keep the family together, but things became extremely difficult. Billy's behavior became overwhelming. The family couldn't understand his behaviors, especially his temper tantrums. Got to the point where they were afraid of him and didn't want to go near him. Mrs. Malama finally agreed to have him admitted to this facility. He hasn't been home since.

That was in 1963, about ten years ago. Billy is, well, almost normal for his age, but is identified as severely retarded with behavior problems. His seizures are now under control. In fact, I believe he hasn't had any for a few years now. His Mom has written him regularly throughout the years. On special occasions like Christmas or his birthday, his oldest sister, Aileen, has sent cards also. We have never heard from his Dad although he was notified of his admission here." She paused and sighed. I remained silent as we walked toward the office looking around at several of the other residents in the room.

"For that matter," Renee continued, "after the first year or so, we hardly hear from any of the families of our people here."

"Is that so," I replied.

"Yeh, but it's reality," she said. "Mrs. Malama is one of the rare ones. In her last letter she expressed that she hasn't been feeling that well lately though, and having to go to the doctor. That's been nearly two months ago. We haven't heard from her since. I usually read her letters to Billy and correspond with her telling her about some of the positive things he does and about his health." She was silent for a minute.

"Now, this program we want to initiate is to see if we can train these severe and acute mentally retarded males to eventually be placed in homes in the community and not live in state operated institutions like this," she said as we reached the office.

"How do we do that?" I asked. She turned and looked at me.

With a bit of urgency and a deep tone in her voice, she said, "That will be your job. That's why we now have a federally funded grant to see if changes can be made through this behavior modification program." We sat down at her desk and she continued.

"You've got your job cut out for you. As you can see, it's not going to be easy. We'll go over the project tomorrow. Today, I want you to familiarize yourself with what's here and also the people, including the staff. There are the records and here's a key to the building. You've seen and waved to some of the staff as we were walking to this office. Introduce yourself to them. They're nice and hard workers." She smiled and added, "We're glad you're here. Like I said, it's not going to be easy but I think it will be rewarding. This behavior modification program has never been tried here before, so do call me whenever you need to. Welcome aboard, Laura, I'm glad you've joined us."

Renee gave me a welcoming hug and left. After a brief look around the office, I went out to meet the staff and familiarize myself to my new work environment.

Billy was one of forty identified as "severely/profoundly retarded"[1] with behavior problems. All of the residents had problems with activities of daily living. This was going to be a big challenge. I soon found out that the staffing might be a problem also. One of the staff members who had been working there for awhile, was resistant to change of the routines. Some had their own ideas of how things should be. Staffing was for 24/7 and there was me, a new hired. I have been in nursing for about ten years, but have never worked with the mentally retarded. Renee stated the project is for two years and required careful monitoring for progress. We have to show positive results. If successful, the program will be initiated for females residents with the similar diagnosis.

After reviewing the planned program and the objectives, preparations were made to start it. Meetings with staff were held to familiarize and instruct everyone what the program was all about, how we would approach it, when we were going to start, and how we would evaluate progress.

The behavior modification program was implemented slowly, but surely. Basically, the goals were to improve behavior and develop basic skills for activities of daily living. Good and positive behaviors are rewarded and bad or negative behaviors are not.

There were forty males in the project—twenty in the control group where no real training was done, and twenty in the training group where the program was implemented. The age range of these males were sixteen to forty years old. One of the first rules was "No clothes no treats; no shoes, no bus rides. M&M candies and/or positive compliments were used as rewards for positive or correct behaviors. It was difficult in the beginning for everyone to be consistent. But slowly it became easier as time passed and the residents responded to the rewards.

Three months after starting the program, although problems exist, positive results were observed. The training group started to present fewer behavior problems than before in all areas. Having observed recognizable improvements were very rewarding to all. The work was mentally, physically, and emotionally draining. I quickly learned the staff needed much leadership, supervision, directions, and flexibility and so did our residents. It was time consuming, tiring, and very challenging. But seeing some positive results were satisfying and everyone appeared happier although sometimes more tired than before the training program started.

A letter came for Billy after the program started. He was excited.

"Mama wite, Mama wite!" he shouted, as he held the letter waving it in front of him.

"Helen give your letter, Billy, you give me letter and I read to you," said Mary, one of the staff on duty.

Billy started to run from her with his letter. He stopped suddenly, then turned.

"Heya, you read," he said as he handed her the letter with a grin. Mary found a chair to sit on and opened the letter as she asked Billy to sit next to her. Billy plopped himself on the floor next to the chair and sat cross-legged. Mary started to read.

"'Dear Billy, I'm so sorry I did not write sooner. Mama loves you very much, but Mama has been sick. I hope you are OK and being a good boy. I hope I can see you someday. Are you eating good? Are you being nice? Tell everybody I say "hello." Remember, I love you very much. Aloha, Your Mama.'"

Billy started clapping. He stood up and jumped up and down for a few seconds.

"Mama wite, Mama wite! Luv you, luv you, she say to me!" he shouted, then ran off to play outside.

Mary put the letter back in the envelope and slipped it in her pocket. She then pulled out another letter addressed to the staff from Billy's Mom that Helen gave her earlier. She read it aloud as I and another staff member, Joan stood nearby.

"Thank you to all of you for taking care of my Billy. I have been very sick and told I have cancer. I don't know how much longer I can write, but will you folks tell Billy every so often that his Mama loves him and will never forget him? Thank you very much. I appreciate all you folks do for him. God bless you all. Thanks again. Aloha, Billy's Mom, Mrs. Malama."

The letter brought tears to our eyes. Mary handed me the letters to be placed in Billy's file and said thoughtfully, "It would be so good if she can see Billy before anything happens to her. Good for them both. Except for pictures, she has never seen Billy grown up." Our gaze met as I nodded. She knew that I thought so too.

After eight months into the program, progress was observed and recorded on all the residents in the training group. Billy no longer took off his shirt at meals and started to use a fork instead of shoveling the food in his mouth with a spoon like most of them did.

Billy was learning to brush his teeth, wash his hands after using the toilet, and combing his hair. Several others learned these skills also. The rate of progress was different for each one, but all in the program looked forward to going for a bus ride each day during the week and all twenty of them looked nicer, neater, and showed improvement in their behavior. The staff was encouraged and happy to see progress in each one of them.

After several months of short bus rides, some staff members were willing to risk extending the bus rides and stop for a short walk in a park before returning to the facility. This activity was carefully planned and extra staff was scheduled on duty.

The first trip was successful but not without problems. As soon as the bus stopped and the door opened, Billy jumped up and ran outside in front of the bus and urinated just outside the bus. Another, couldn't wait to go either and wet his pants in the bus. In our planning, we failed to see that stopping for a walking activity meant another ten minutes on the bus before toileting. To some of them, it made a big difference.

After Billy had urinated, he was so excited, he ran off ahead of the group. Briefly, he was lost but his shouting for "Mama" helped staff find him. That was the beginning of many excursions and other "risky" activities. However, they were great learning and teaching experiences for all of us including the public. People at first, stared or glared at us and quickly hastened their steps or crossed the street to get away from us. But now a few weeks later, they have started smiling and waving back especially to Billy who enjoyed waving his hands and saying "Hi!" or "'loha!." We were elated with their progress. We were also happy that the public was more accepting and friendlier.

By August, many of the behavior problems had decreased. Positive or good behaviors took their place. Bowel movement and urine accidents had dropped considerably. All were using the fork and/or spoon properly. Bibs were replaced by napkins at meals and all were drinking from a cup without many spills. The noise level in the building had decreased and the music played in the building could now be easily heard.

Some improved their vocabulary by speaking more words and being able to express their needs or pointing to their needs. Many learned to say "plise" or "puhleze" for "please." Billy learned to ask for something he wanted. "Plise like dis" he'd say while pointing to what he wanted instead of just grabbing the item. "Tank you, no like," he'd say if you offered him something he didn't want instead of hitting your hand or pushing it away. As the stress level at work dropped, so did mine. Everyone was more relaxed, cooperative, and happier. We were all pleased with the progress made including the administration.

It was the beginning of September that we heard from Billy's family again. His sister, Aileen wrote, and there was a short note from his Mom.

"I love you, Billy. I'll always love you. Be good and always remember your Mama. Say "aloha" to everybody, okay?"

Aileen's letter stated that their Mom was quite ill and undergoing cancer treatments. The doctors weren't sure if she was going to make it till Thanksgiving. Billy was told only that his Mom was very sick.

On an impulse, I turned to Billy and asked, "Billy, you want to go see your Mama? Do you?"

"Go see Mama? Yaa, I go see my Mama. I like go see my Mama," he grinned.

"OK, let's see what we can do so you can go see your Mama," I said. "But remember, you have to be good boy, okay?"

"Okay," he answered, "I be goo-boy" nodding his head.

Much planning and arrangements had to be done for this to happen. Billy's Mom lived on another island. Mary looked at Billy and saw the little boy his Mom probably remembers.

"I'll take you to go see your Mama, Billy. You be good boy and I'll take you to go see your Mama," Mary said. She then reached out and gave Billy a hug.

Billy grinned from ear to ear and said, "Luv Mama, go see Mama. Tank you." Unexpectedly, he gave Mary a quick hug and ran outside to ride the swings.

Mary then turned to me and said, "We have to do it, we have to take him to see his Mom on Lanai before anything happens."

I agreed and we started to make plans for this to happen. I knew Mary was very competent and responsible and could take care of Billy outside the facility. Much thought and preparation was done. The date was set for November 10. His family was notified so they could prepare for his visit home also. Mary was excited, happy, and maybe even a little apprehensive about accompanying Billy for the trip, but more than willing to do it.

On November 10, at seven a.m., Mary and Billy drove off to the Honolulu International Airport from Pearl City. Billy wore a new aloha shirt that the staff bought for him and bermuda shorts. Matching socks with a pair of polished brown shoes completed his outfit. I wondered how long he would keep his shoes on. He looked handsome with his hair neatly combed back and a smile on his face, even with a missing tooth. Billy was overjoyed to learn he was going to ride the airplane to see his Mama.

I think we all prayed silently as they had departed, hoping things would work out well without any incidents or problems. Everyone anticipated their return that afternoon.

At 3:45 p.m. I looked outside the window to see if Mary's car was visible. Their flight back was expected to land at 2:55 p.m. Arrival time on Lanai was nine-thirty that morning and Aileen was picking them up from the airport. They were spending the morning with Mrs. Malama and Aileen at the hospital and later planned to have lunch with Aileen, her family, and sisters at home. Then, Aileen had planned a short sight-seeing trip of the island before returning to the airport.

Mary's car was nowhere in sight yet. The day shift staff lingered. We all waited anxiously. The minutes dragged. It was now 4:05p.m.

Finally, at 4:20, Mary's car was spotted coming around the bend. Before long, the car stopped in front of the building as we gathered outside to greet them. Out came Billy as soon as Mary stopped the car.

Grinning from ear to ear, he shouted, "I see Mama. I see Mama an Aiyeen too, an my oda sistas." He ran toward the group. "Mama see me," he said pointing to himself.

"Mama sick. She in bed," he added somewhat sadly. "She say she luv me. I kiss Mama. Mama kiss, hug me too. I see Aiyeen baby too. But Mama tiyed. She only stay in bed. I say I luv you, Mama. Mama say she luv me too, an tell me I big boy now." He paused thoughtfully, then off he went to ride the swings smilingly.

We all stood watching him as moisture filled our eyes. Renee was there with us smiling. She was pleased. We both gave Mary a hug. "Thank you so much, Mary," I said, voice cracking, "you and everyone made this possible. I'm so glad Mrs. Malama was able to see her Billy."

"Mrs. Malama was overjoyed too," said Mary happily.

Loretta

---

[1]   The American Medical Association Home Medical Encyclopedia, pg.678.

TRUE FRIENDS

True friends
Will never change,

No matter what happens
They're still the same:

Always caring, uplifting
And sharing

Their sorrows and joys
Either big ones—or small . . .

And who ever has
A friend like that

Is richly blessed
For the rest of his life.

Lana

MISINFORMATION CENTRAL

My grandmother was a great believer in work being the cure of all ills. Her motto was, "If you do the dos, you won't have time to do the don'ts."

I suppose that was the problem with Nelly Decker, not enough dos to keep her mind, and mouth, occupied and out other people's business.

Nelly was the pursed-mouth, self-righteous housekeeper of our next-door neighbor, Mrs. Pierson. "Miz Decker", as the local merchants called her, kept a starched and polished house for the sweet spirited Scandinavian septuagenarian. She did the simple cooking, cleaning and shopping. This still did not keep her busy enough to avoid the don'ts.

It was common knowledge that Nelly listened in on every party-line telephone call that tinkled her bell. How? She picked up the receiver on every ring and unashamedly added her opinions to conversations not intended for her ears When she was confronted about it, she took an injured tone and stated she thought the call was for her. No one ever did call her because anything said to her became seed for Nelly's latest crop of gossip, which she freely scattered as she went about her weekly shopping. She seemed oblivious to the citizens of our small community fleeing before her whenever possible like roaches avoiding a bright light. She just raised her volume if no one remained in discreet hearing range.

Mrs. Pierson's home was always immaculate and we all wondered how Nelly had time to keep it that way. Her information, and sometimes misinformation, gathering would put any governmental agency to shame. The phone was her main source of tidbits about what people were saying. She had a graduated means of determining what they were doing. Pristine, heavily starched lace curtains allowed her a three-quarter view of the neighborhood, which encompassed most of the town except for the Main Street business block. Any movement by neighbors was observed through the eyelets of the draperies, betrayed only by a slight twitch of the folds.

If there were cars parked on the street to hinder the lacy view, it suddenly became essential that Mrs. Pierson's rugs receive a thorough shaking from the front porch. The back porch only provided a view of an empty field bordering the river. If the action on the street was sustained for more than a minute or two, the rugs were in danger of having tufts shaken out of them. To further endanger the rugs, activity on down the street or of longer duration brought about furious shaking at the curb. A wedding at the church in the next block resulted in the need for a whole new set of rugs.

Nelly was no more shy about asking nosy questions than she was about passing on her take of any given situation.

My father was hired for a job out of town which required him to be gone all through the week, only coming home on weekends. When he had the opportunity to work some overtime, he missed the weekend trip home. His boss, grateful for his help, offered the use of the unfurnished basement in his home to avoid the cost of a rented room elsewhere.

Nelly, living up to her reputation, asked my mother if my father had left her permanently. Mom's Nelly-tolerance was very limited and she allowed flippancy to get the better of her.

"No, he's still coming home. When he takes his bed, I'll know he's gone for good."

On the next trip home, Dad loaded a table, chair, some pots and pans and a recliner in his truck. Before the mattress was completely loaded, the party-line was buzzing with the *news* that Red and Beth had finally split up. Fortunately, townspeople knew better and also knew the source of the don'ts.

JoLynne

NEVER TOO LATE TO LEARN

An auspicious fortune cookie message told me, "You will have a potential urge." At forty-five years old, I had an urge to finally decide what I wanted to be when I grew up. With a lot of encouragement from a mentor and loving friends, I left my job, sold my house and packed my little car to go away to college. I am not sure which was most unprepared—a middle-aged college student or a small Christian college in California accustomed to teenaged students. For both of us, some adjustments were necessary.

Imagine what it is like for a woman of my age living in a dorm at her daughter's Alma Mater.

First, some of the professors remembered my daughter and expected me to follow in her footsteps. What is wrong with this picture?

Living in a dorm with 18 and 19 year olds was a culture shock of major proportions. I'm sure for the teenagers, it was like having an elephant in the living room. They carefully circled me, avoiding contact, but trying to decide what to make of me. The school administration decided I would be a good roommate for students who didn't fit anywhere else. As a consequence, I had a cross-cultural education. Over the three years I was there, my roommates were from such diverse cultures as Japanese, Peruvian, Chinese, Native American, Cambodian and South Central Los Angeles.

I finally became accepted in the dorm when I began baking and selling chocolate chip cookies to fellow students as a means of making a little spending money. Some classmates even forgot that I was the oldest student on campus.

Being a mature student was an advantage for me. The classes were more interesting and pertinent to me than to many of the younger students. I had some life experience by which to evaluate what I was learning. Not being distracted by the dating game was an advantage in doing well on exams. To be involved in a fuller experience of college, I became the start-up editor-in-chief of the college's first newspaper. The only problem with that was falling asleep in class after pulling an all-nighter to get the paper ready for print.

I was thrilled to have family and friends from four states come to see me graduate. But then, I was faced with the usual cold shower of reality—job-hunting time!

I began working in a group home with gang girls from Los Angeles, another culture shock. However, not all the girls were gang members. One was a boat-person from Vietnam, surviving horrendous experiences to join her father in this country only to discover he had founded a new family and had no place for her in his life. Another of the girls was the sole survivor when soldiers burned her home in San Salvador.

These experiences pulled at my heartstrings and helped prepare me for a second job in a community-counseling center for immigrants and refugees. I had the privilege of working with people from all over the world, from Iran to the Sudan, from Tobago to Turkey. This allowed me insights into cultures I had never heard of in my midwestern upbringing. Although I loved my work, I am too much of a small-town person to adapt to the fast paced lifestyle of Southern California. When the opportunity came to move to Wyoming, I again packed my little car, pulled up my shallow roots and drove to the Rocky Mountains of Wyoming.

I began working there in a state youth treatment center with adolescents who were court-ordered into treatment for being in trouble with the law. Most of them had come from homes that were abusive. Again my age was an advantage and the kids began to see me as a surrogate grandmother of sorts, which allowed them to talk out their problems with me.

I soon learned I needed specific education to help them more effectively. As a consequence, I began the 600 mile round trip to Denver every weekend for two years to get a master's degree in Clinical Social Work.

Two months before I graduated, the governor, in his finite wisdom, decided to cut the state budget by closing the center. He put 60 people out of work and scattered the residents to whatever fate awaited them.

With a brand new degree and no job, I consented to a job interview back in Arizona and the rest of the story, as they say, is history.

This has all been a long way of telling you that I am what I decided I wanted to be when I grew up—a counselor. Now, I'm waiting for another fortune cookie message to be fulfilled. It said, "You should presently begin to play with a full deck."

JoLynne

AN ILL WIND

Whap! Another shingle smacked the air conditioner and flew off the roof, on its way to Mexico, I surmised. The wind was fierce, blowing damnedably cold since early evening and gathering strength at bedtime. Sleep, when it came, was punctuated with bad dreams and ominous sounds. The jarring brrrang of the doorbell was like the scream of a tortured animal to my disturbed half-conscious thoughts.

The noise persisted, bringing me fully awake. I pulled my heavy robe on and pushed my feet into the slippers by my bed. I called out, "Who is it? Who's there? I'm coming—just a minute—I'm coming."

I switched on the entry light. Peering through the peephole of my front door I saw a young woman, a girl, really, shivering as she continued pressing the doorbell. She was not dressed for the cold, in fact she had no wrap at all.

Cautiously I opened the door with the screen still shut. No vehicle or other persons were in sight.

She cried out, "Please—I'm freezing. Please let me in."

I pushed the screen open and took her arm to pull her in. She stumbled on the entry and nearly fell on the stepdown to my living room. Her teeth were chattering. Motioning her to the recliner, she collapsed into it. I grabbed the afghan off the sofa and wrapped it doubled over her.

Between sobs and gasps for breath she squeaked out, "Thank you. You saved my life."

It was tempting to say, "Oh, it was nothing," but I was too bewildered by this creature to be so flip. Instead I asked, "What is your name and whatever are you doing out on this dreadful night? No—wait. Let me make you a cup of tea and when you are calm we'll talk."

She just nodded.

Thank goodness for microwaves. She had the mug of tea in her hands in no more than three minutes. She smiled and meekly asked, "May I have some sugar?"

She took two big spoonfuls out of the bowl I set by her.

From the chair opposite I inspected my unplanned visitor. Honey blonde hair was cut in a kind of wedge with a startling streak of pink on one side. The blue cotton sweater she wore was ripped at the shoulder seam. Mascara made dark trails on her cheeks and a pink lipstick smear gave her the countenance of a sad clown. The high-heeled silver sandals on her feet were missing one heel. She looked no more than sixteen.

The fake antique clock on my mantle chimed eleven p.m.

"Okay, Sugar Plum, who the hell are you to be wandering about on this hellacious night?"

She looked astonished by my harsh words, but I was in no mood for niceties.

"He . . . he tried . . . I ran . . . oh, I'm so sorry . . ." Her voice trailed off and she again burst into tears.

All right, this is a baby, I thought, she's not used to confrontation. I softened my approach. "Look, just tell me your name."

"Tiffany . . . Tiffany Albright. I went to this party, see, with my friend Amanda. We were going to meet the guys there. My folks don't like Jude, so they wouldn't have let me go if they'd known he would be there. So I was, like, just going to have, like, you know, fun at the party. It was no big deal. The music was already loud when I got there and the kids were, like, you know, dancing and hanging out. Donny grabbed me and we started dancing. It didn't mean anything. He was just, like, you know, one of the party."

(Her "you knows" were irritating, but she was on a roll, so I didn't interrupt her.)

"When Jude came in he saw me with Donny and jerked me away. I explained that it didn't mean anything. He sort of backed off.

"There were lots of sodas on the kitchen counter, but Jude pulled a bottle of Everclear out of his coat pocket and poured half a glass that he topped off with Sprite. He took a long swallow and insisted I have some too. When I pushed it away he got mad.

"Donny said, 'Hey, man, don't force her if she don't want it.'

"Jude got in his face and yelled, 'Get your own babe, this one's mine. I'll do what I damn well please with what's mine.'

"He took another gulp of the booze then slapped me hard and pushed the glass to my mouth. I guess I was, like, too shocked by his hitting me to resist. I nearly choked as he forced me to drink.

"'That's more like it,' he said. 'Now let's have some fun. That's what I came for.'"

"He pulled me to the middle of the floor and began to dance. The loud music was going all the time, but the others had stopped moving and were just staring at us.

"'What's the matter with you people? It's a party. Get with it!'

"Brandon, Donny's best friend, said, 'Jude, just chill—we all want to have fun, but it's not cool to be slapping a girl.'

"Jude shoved me against a chair and I landed on the floor. His face was red. He grabbed Brandon's shirt and screamed, 'What the f—has it to do with you? You think you can tell me how I should handle a bitch?'

"That's when he hit Brandon with his fist. Blood spurted from his nose. I think he went down, but Jude yanked me off the floor, tearing my sweater. He yelled, 'We're outta here, bitch. Come on!'

"Donny and another guy got in front of him and pulled me away. Amanda screamed, 'Get out, Tiff! Run for your life! He's gone crazy!'

"So I ran out and kept running. But I, like, got lost and it's so cold, and I didn't know where I was, and branches kept falling off trees—and I went up to one house, but nobody answered. Then a branch hit me and knocked me down and my heel broke off my shoe . . . and . . . and . . ."

At that point a fresh flow of tears and sobs interrupted her tale of woe.

"Who are your folks, Tiffany? Where do you live?"

Broken up by sobs, she managed to get out, "South of town. Will you call my folks? No—wait—they're going to be mad. I don't know what to do. I was supposed to be home by eleven."

"You must call your parents. I'm sure they are worried about you."

Hail began a rat-a-tat on the roof at the same time a car sped past on the street. Seconds later, another vehicle, well past the speed limit flashed by.

I picked up my phone and asked Tiffany for her parents' number. While I punched in the numbers she gave me, the screech of brakes sounded out front. Almost simultaneously I heard approaching police sirens in the neighborhood. Something intuitive warned me of danger. Tossing the phone to Tiffany, I jumped to the door and threw the deadbolt in place.

A car door slammed and seconds later banging on the screen was accompanied by a man's voice shouting, "Tiffany, you're in there. I know it. You got me into this shit. Come out or I'll break this door down or burn the place to the ground. You hear me? I'll do it! Who you with in there? You got another guy who wants to take me on? I'll cut him up just like I did Donny and Brandon! Open up!"

Tiffany had sprung from the chair and stood terrified, looking from me to the door. She held the phone with a shaking hand and I could barely hear a voice on the line calling her name.

Tiffany hissed, "It's him. It's Jude! He's come to kill me. Oh, God. Oh, God! Don't let him in. How did he find me? I don't even know where I am."

I took the phone out of her hand and put it to my ear. "Are you Tiffany's parents?"

"Yes. Who are you? Where is she?"

"I'm Constance Milton at 1542 Bella Drive. Tiffany's here with me, but you need to come for her as soon as you possibly can. We are being threatened by an intruder named Jude."

"Oh, my Lord," was the response. "That young man is unstable and probably on drugs. We'll be there as soon as we can. Don't let him in."

The screen door was jerked aside and Jude pounded on the solid door. "Open up, damn it! I'll break this door down."

I shouted, "Tiffany, help me move this chair and jam it against the door. Then I'll call the police."

Suddenly police sirens were directly in front of the house, even as I was attempting to punch 911. A second car's brakes squealed at the curb. Pushing the drape aside from the window, I saw the hail had turned to slicing rain. A man was spread-eagled on the wet walkway, two police officers standing over him. The narrow residential street seemed full of vehicles; three police cars and the two others unfamiliar to me. A pair of officers were standing by two young men who gesticulated wildly.

The raucous noise of the doorbell added to what felt, for all the world, like a nightmare unleashed.

Leaning over the chair we'd jammed against the door, I could barely see through the peephole. A uniformed police officer stood waiting while water poured down his neck from the overhead eave. I pulled the chair away and opened the door.

"May I come in, Ma'am?"

"P-p-please, please do," I stuttered.

"I'm officer Gardena. Is this young lady Tiffany Albright?"

Tiffany nodded.

"Ma'am, you own this residence? You are Constance Milton?"

"Yes, I am."

"We are investigating an assault incident that took place not far from here, involving Miss Albright. We'll take your statement and leave you in peace. Miss Albright needs to come with us.

"Tiffany finally regained her wits and her voice to ask, "What did he do to Donny and Brandon? He said he 'cut' them."

"Miss, two young men were injured and are getting medical attention. That's all I can say at this time. Do you have a coat? The weather's really bad out there."

"Can we wait for my Mom and Dad? They said they're coming right away."

"Well, we can wait while I take Ms Milton's statement."

"How did Jude find me here?"

"He said he drove all over the neighborhood until his headlights reflected off a silver heel from the shoes you were wearing. It was on the sidewalk out front."

The next half hour was anticlimax. Tiffany's parents arrived, thanked me, and said they'd be in touch. They drove with their daughter to police headquarters.

The young men in the second car were friends of the injured youths and determined to stop Jude from hurting Tiffany, so they followed him after notifying the police.

I finally fell asleep sometime after one o'clock, with the sounds of the storm lessening.

It was all over the paper the next morning with the arrest of Jude on drug charges as well as "assault with a deadly weapon." His victims were released after treatment for knife lacerations.

The windstorm damage was extensive, but took second page to the "party" news.

Mary

AN OLD FOLKS HOME

Once young, productive, and vibrant were they,
Instead, forlorn, wrinkled and gray, they quietly lay.
A few with their canes, they slowly go walking,
Many are sitting, watching, listening, or simply rocking.

Some happily strolling in and out of the hallways,
Others with walkers, barely make it through doorways.
Those in wheelchairs move slowly along,
Join their peers in activities where they feel they belong.

For some they are there, no family to care,
While others, for family, a burden too hard to bear.
Some there for short term physical rehabilitation,
But, most reside there for long term habitation.

From many walks of life, they're committed for care,
Some sad, but accepting, some in despair.
Many confused not knowing where they are,
While others are happy and shine like a star.

Several whose memories no longer exist,
Challenge the best for their care, to endure and persist.
Then there are those whose seasons are ending,
And soon, from this earth they will be departing.

Loretta

ROSES FOR A FALLEN SOLDIER

No time for roses, no place to plant
His blood was spread instead of that.
His eyes were looking into space
Which is unknown and very far,
To those alive and still apart
Of a World, that is a greater Mess!

Forgive us, friend, we have to leave.
We'll pass the message to your wife.
Don't worry friend, she'll hear the truth.
That you've been brave, and died for love,
For land that you thought was the best
Then she will plant a field of roses,
Oh, roses, roses of greater quest!

Tatiana

MISSING YOU

An empty chair, across the table
One cup of coffee and a plate for one . . .
I am missing you.
A couple walks on the street, holding hands . . .
I swallow my tears, I am missing you.
Coffee Shop at lunch, waitress offers a booth
I shake my head. Booth too big for one.
She glances into my eyes, my eyes are red. She understands,
She seems to be missing someone too.
She leads me to a dark corner, a tiny table for one . . .
We exchange a glance with eyes full of tears,
She wipes her's. I wipe mine as we both try to smile.
At night my bed is empty, the pillow next to mine is cold.
I put my face against the pillow, trying to hold my sobs,
But the tears are running, running . . .
If only you knew, how much, how much, I am missing you.

Tatiana

GRANDMA SAID . . .

Born of a little raisin of an Englishwoman and a good-looking dandy of an Irishman, my grandmother was a curious mix of personalities. A whimsical streak of Irish mischievousness was tempered by a wide band of English stoicism and practicality.

Grandma was a teetotaling Methodist who never allowed herself to complain, about anything. The closest she came to talking about poor health was to say, "I had a bad spell last month, but I'm better now." This same person delighted in teaching her grandchildren to knit, embroider, garden and how to make homemade Cracker Jacks. She allowed us to play King-of-the-Mountain on her large hassock in the middle of the living room. She was unflappable when the inevitable bumps and bruises caused tears, and even when my brother split his head open on the plaster Scottie dog doorstop.

The best thing about Grandma, after her hugs and bottomless cookie jar, was her ability to offer the perfect response to everything. When she was greeted with, "Eithel, how are you today?" she always responded, "I'm as fine as frog hair." When someone was self-denigrating about her own appearance, the reassurance was, "You can't tell on a galloping horse." Although this usually caused laughter, or at least a distraction, there was a mild underlying rebuke. Implied was, "If you are busy enough, no one is going to notice." A litany of petty complaints was brought to a halt with, "Is it going to matter in a hundred years?"

An endless supply of down home-isms served as subtle education regarding proper lady-like behavior. Chewing ice from a cold drink was "like a pig eating coal," *not* a good thing. "Whistling girls and barking dogs always come to bad ends," left no doubt what Grandma thought. Rising early, working hard and not gossiping were essential virtues. Failure at any of these brought silent, but unmistakable censure.

In spite of not openly criticizing neighbors, the meaning was clear when Grandma made such statements as, "He is as honest as the Hartzers"; "she is just like Nelly Decker"; or a person "works as hard as Bud Moody." It was common knowledge in our small town that the Hartzers bought paint, used it, and then refilled the cans with water before returning them for a refund. Nelly Decker had a reputation as a champion nosy gossip, and Bud Moody was known to be so lazy he wouldn't scratch where it itches.

Grandma regularly attended church, but did not push her faith on anyone. She never discussed politics and avoided conflicts, usually defusing them with one of her pithy expressions. She only used profanity once. When tired of hearing her three teenage sons blaspheming, she showed them that it didn't sound very nice.

Her best-remembered and most practical advice to her grandchildren was a mixture of Irish wit and English practicality. It echoes in my mind decades after I first heard it. I even *try* to live by the words, "If you do all the dos, you won't have time for the don'ts."

Thank you, Grandma.

JoLynne

THE HILL

He drove too fast
Up on the hill,
Along the winding road
That had no end in sight . . .

She closed her eyes,
Afraid to look
At mountain rocky side
That went straight down
Some thousand feet
And may be more, indeed,

But then she heard
The engine hollow sound,
And in no time
Their car began to slide . . .

The wheels have lost
Its grip upon the road
And in a while, their car
Went tumbling down . . .

The last thing she recalled
Was great big bang
And nothing else at all . . .

Lana

THE GIRLS

Waves of conflicting emotions threatened to swamp me as I looked around the group enjoying wine and canapés in my sunset-filled Arizona room. These women are as, no . . . more familiar to me than my own blood sisters, and yet I felt unsettled, restless.

We have been meeting twice a month in one another's homes for at least twenty years. Our "newbie", Gwen, has only been part of the group for twelve years. We know all about each others' families, relationships, hardships and challenges. We celebrate birthdays and the arrival of grand and great grandchildren. We have mourned with those who lost spouses, went through divorce, a son killed in battle, a granddaughter dead from a car accident. We've been through all the ups and downs with one another. I listened to the chattering voices around me, catching snippets of conversation.

". . . believe me, I thought I was going to scream when the nurse made me get out of bed."

"You really should go to see Dr. K., he's done wonders for . . ."

". . . changing pharmacies, they've raised the price . . ."

"This pain, right here, is so . . ."

I escaped to the kitchen for more lemonade and leaned against the counter, trying to analyze my confused thoughts. Why as I feeling so dissatisfied, so . . . unfulfilled? The murmur of voices clouded my thinking even more, so I took my muddled head to the bathroom.

The sudden quiet took away any excuses for not thinking this out. These are all good friends, trustworthy and true. I realized I wasn't liking them very much at the moment, but could not say why I was so disturbed.

Gwen had retired from teaching high school English and Literature. Sally, good ol' Sal, had been a major in the Army and then worked for the State Department. Roberta had been a civil servant, a G.S. muckety-muck equivalent to a two-star general. Lindy retired from corporate life where she had been a comptroller. Paula was the artist in our midst who still made a considerable living with her paintings and jewelry. Patricia, not Patty or Trisha, had used her degree in botany to become the director of a nearby nature conservancy. I had sold my employment agency for a very comfortable retirement. There was not a slouch, a nitwit, among us, if I do say so myself.

Why, then, why the annoyance, the shredded nerves? As I thought about what I had overheard of the conversations, it became clear. All of us, the youngest of us sixty-three years old, were spending all of our time together hashing and rehashing our aches, pains and illnesses. What a way to spend, not only our precious time together, but the rest of our dwindling years!

Being a problem-solver, my next thought was, "What can I do about it?" These friends are too precious for me to just drop them. Everyone needs all the friends they have. We each have gifts and abilities to share, even if we can't be as physically active as we once were. Ideas began to drop, one by one, like water from the leaky faucet I hadn't fixed yet.

Just as I shoved the bathroom door open, Sal knocked on it. I almost knocked her over.

"Are you all right, Pam? We were getting concerned since you were gone so long," Sal inquired.

"I'm suddenly terrific," I answered, and had no chance to explain, since in typical Sal fashion, she had a bawdy remark to make.

"That doesn't deserve a comment, Sal," I groaned. "Come on, I want to talk to the girls."

Twenty minutes later, after a short silence while they mulled over my monologue, chatter again broke out.

Gwen said, "I think a book club/discussion group would be good and I'd be willing to organize it."

"I know some great people who would be glad to talk to us about estate planning and handling our finances," Lindy offered.

Patricia chimed in with, "I know where there are some great gardens their owners would be happy to let us visit."

"I was just thinking the other day that I should do something with all the slides I took during my travels all over the world. How about some armchair traveling?" Sal's offer was greeted with as much enthusiasm as the other ideas.

The talk, with ideas popping up here and there, continued for quite a while.

"Okay, are we all agreed on this? One person will host our meeting, coordinated with a volunteer to provide the topic, to change each month." Approval was enthusiastically unanimous.

Sal's drill sergeant voice overcame the resulting chatter.

"And our talk about our aches and pains and pills will be limited. We will set a timer to end our organ recitals after 15 minutes. Anyone who violates that condition will take us all out to dinner!"

The laughter that followed washed away the last of my dis-ease.

JoLynne

COMING HOME

The sky was overcast, gloomy and gray. Rosaria's mood was no different. Her work day had started at the Naval Recreation Center. She was a janitress and was sweeping the area this morning.

For the past few days, she was thinking about her son, Felix, for it's been nearly six months since she heard from him. It was Mother's Day when she last received a call. He told her that he was in Los Angeles and wished her a "Happy Mother's Day." He also told her work was slow, but not to worry. He was OK, and he'd try to call her more often. When she asked him why doesn't he come home and find a job on Oahu or one of the outside islands. "Maybe," he said, "but not now. Don't worry, Mama. I love you and I'll call you again," he added. She remembered telling him she loved him also and to be careful. Then they said goodbye. Two days later she received a Mother's Day card from him. That was the last she had heard from him.

Over a year ago, he and his wife were divorced. Things just didn't work out. Their three young children were with their mother. Several months after the divorce, he left the islands and went to California. At first, Rosaria had heard from her son about once a month. Needless to say, she was now worried.

She went about doing her cleaning chores mechanically, her thoughts miles away. She prayed he would come home soon or that she would at least hear from him. For the past few weeks, she had been thinking about his life. Yes, he was a bit spoiled being the youngest and only boy. Practically everyone catered to his wants and needs. He didn't do as well as his sisters did in school.

He joined the Navy soon after he graduated from high school. After basic training and some technical training, he eventually was assigned to an aircraft carrier. He loved traveling and enjoyed his assignment. After he married and started his family, Rosaria thought he would settle down. He did for awhile, but apparently things didn't work He enjoyed going out and having a good time with his buddies and liked gambling also. Rosaria knew that these were some reasons his wife divorced him after years of marriage and three children.

He had been gone for over a year and a half. She hoped he would come home and give up some of his undesirable habits. She also hoped he would spend some time with his children and settle down. This is what she prayed for.

This morning, she felt discouraged, helpless, and even hopeless. All of a sudden, she stopped her sweeping and undeterred by her surroundings, she cried out pleadingly, "Oh God, please let him come home!" As she stood there, head bowed, shoulders drooped, and eyes closed, she felt a warm sensation encompass her body and sensed a light present. She opened her eyes. There in front of her was a bright ray of light. It was there but a few seconds, and then it disappeared. It was once again gray and gloomy.

The experience left Rosaria in awe, but she felt peace instead of sadness. She was able to perform her responsibilities without feeling as she did earlier and the rest of the day went smoothly.

After work, Rosaria rode the bus home as usual and thought about her day, especially that ray of light. Now there was some sunlight through the clouds and she felt encouraged and hopeful.

She walked home after getting off the bus. The walk was refreshing. She was greeted by her grandchildren when she reached her gate.

The unexpected and grievous death of her husband four years before was difficult for the family, but especially for her. Four months prior to his death, a daughter passed away having suffered from post-partum depression. She was glad that her younger daughter, Lucia, her husband Matt, and their two children moved back to the islands to stay with her soon after her husband's funeral.

Nearly two years ago, Lucia had a new baby girl. She was a blessing especially for Rosaria. Uplifted emotionally with her new granddaughter, she was able to overcome her periods of sadness and depression gradually as she spent more time with the baby and the older children helping to meet their needs also.

That evening, after her usual chores and some time with the family, Rosaria decided to go to bed earlier than usual. She felt exhausted, and it didn't take her long to fall asleep soundly. Even the children's playing did not waken her.

The next morning, while she prepared for work, Lucia informed her Mother that Helen and Ben, her oldest daughter and son-in law, were coming over shortly and needed to talk with her.

"Why dey coming?" she asked in broken English. Growing up in a foreign country and speaking her native language most of the time, Rosaria learned some English after her children started going to school. Like most of the people in the islands, pidgin or broken English is spoken more commonly at home.

"I not sure, Mama." replied Lucia.

"Why you not shua? You don know? Dey no come dis early befo," she said. *"You shua you don know?"* she asked suspiciously. *"Maybe you know, but you no like tell me. No lie,"* she added.

"I don't know, Mama. But last night, there was a phone call for you from Los Angeles. You were sound asleep. They couldn't tell me anything, but they gave me a number to call in the morning. So I called Helen and told her about the phone call. She said she would call for you this morning. And afterwards, she and Ben would come and stop by before they go to work," Lucia replied. She did not want to disclose to her Mom that it was the LAPD that had called the night before and that the number they had given to call back in the morning was for the morgue.

"I tink iss about yo Brudda," Rosaria said. She paused and added, *"I know iss about him. I hope he not in jail."* She lowered her head, sighed, then turned and walked toward the stove. *"Well, I guess you betta make some coffee fo yo Sista,"* she said.

Lucia turned when she heard her daughter. She was thankful that two years old Sarah got up and came into the kitchen.

"Hi, Momma, 'lo Nana!" as she embraced her Mom. Sarah then went to her Nana and also gave her a hug.

"Good morning, Honey! Did you sleep good?"

"Yep," said Sarah.

"Want some toast for breakfast?" asked Lucia.

"Yep, an wit jelly," she replied.

"OK. Nana's having that too with some coffee. Do you want hot chocolate, Sarah?"

"Oh, ya, Momma," she replied, nodding her head.

Shortly after, Lucia heard some noise outside, looked out the window and saw her sister getting out of out of their car. She hurriedly went to open the door and welcomed Helen and Ben in. "It's so good to see you both," she said. Before she could say any more, Rosaria came to greet them also.

"*Hallo, Annaco*," said Rosaria, "*Comosta, cayo?*" Before they could answer, she asked, "*You telepone ol ready?*" directing her question to Helen.

Realizing that it was best to tell her Mom everything now, Helen replied, "Yes, Mama, I called. It was the police department in Los Angeles that called last night, but this morning, the number they gave, I found out, was the morgue. They have Fel . . ."

"*I know it. I know iss about yo Brudda,*" Rosaria interrupted. "*Awan iti biag nan—he dead, huh? Natayen, iso imbaga da, huh?*" she anxiously asked sitting at the edge of her chair. Then asked again, "*He dead, das wat dey say, huh?*"

"Yes, Mama, he's dead. He was found in a warehouse that had burned down in the city, but they couldn't identify him right away," said Helen.

"*Wat you mean? Dey don know him? Wen he die?*" Rosaria asked, her voice a little quieter and her eyes wider, starting to fill with tears.

"Mama, the building burned down about six months ago they said, and they didn't know who he was," Helen started to explain.

"*Wat yo mean, dey don know him?*" Rosaria questioned again, with some resentment in her voice as she stood up.

"Mama, listen," Helen continued. "He was burned so badly they didn't know who he was. Even his ID was burned. They were going to bury him as a 'John Doe' if they couldn't identify his dental plates, but they finally did yesterday. Mama, when they don't know who a person is, they just name them 'John Doe' and that's what they were going to do to Felix. If they didn't find out who he was by the end of yesterday, they were just going to bury him as 'John Doe.' They took long to identify him because they didn't know where he came from until a few days ago. Three days ago, the police finally got a lead to check Hawaii. A detective flew to here and was able to find the dentist that identified his teeth plates yesterday. Do you understand, Mama?" she asked, as she put her arm around her Mom's shoulder.

"*You mean only yestaday dey know who him? Dey bring his teet and dey know him?*" asked Rosaria.

"No, Mama, they bring his teeth marks and it matched the teeth marks his dentist had of him," Helen explained.

"Ohhh," said Rosaria. She was quiet for a moment as she sat down again, then asked, "*Wat time dey do dat yestaday?*" as she dried her tears.

"Do what? You mean when they identified the teeth marks?" Helen replied.

"Yeh, wat time dey fine out?" questioned Rosaria.

"They said in the morning, but they didn't tell me what time. I don't know, Mom," said Helen. If you want to know, maybe we can find out."

"I'll call and find out," said Lucia. She had been quiet all this time but felt that it was important for her mother to know. She quickly went into the living room and called the morgue. Except for the children eating their breakfast, everyone sat quietly, waiting anxiously. In a few minutes, Lucia rejoined them in the kitchen.

"What did they say?" Helen asked.

"It was about 1:40 in the afternoon in Los Angeles, when the detective called the the morgue. According to the detective's report, it was about 10:30 in the morning here when his dental plates were identified by the dentist. Also, they want to know what the next of kin would like to do with his remains. They need to know within the next 24 hours," reported Lucia.

Everyone was quiet. Rosaria looked at her daughters. Thoughts went through her mind. She had never dreamed that she would live to bury two of her children. Now less than five years later, she will be burying her only son. Why, what went wrong, she wondered. I should be the one to go before my children, she thought as tears rolled down her cheeks.

"Mama," Helen said, as she held her Mama close, "Mama, I guess you don't have to decide right now, but later today . . ."

"No, I know now. He coming home. He haf to come home to his family," she said. *"I no like he be alone someplace I don know. Yeh, he's coming home. Call dem back now. Tell dem to sen him home soon."*

"All right, Mama," said Lucia, "I'll call them back and let them know."

Rosaria recalled the events at work the day before . . . that gloomy day when the ray of shining light appeared in front of her so miraculously. She realized it was about the same time when her son's dental plates were identified. Her prayers were answered not as she had hoped, but none the less, he was coming home.

Loretta

THE DIGGERS

They are digging for something
In my neighborhood yard
With a drill and machinery
Working day and night

But when I ask
What are they trying to find
Digging so deep
And with all their might,

They look at me, as if I am blind:
"We look for the essence and meaning of life,
They told us, it must be right here,—
Buried alive . . ."

Lana

PLACES

PLACES

ELEPHANT TRUMPET

The chatter of monkeys outside the window wakened me, my fourth day in Kenya. My roommate Cheryl, a young naturalist from Tempe, Arizona, was already up and dressed.

"Hey, sleepyhead, aren't you interested in bagging a rhinoceros today?" she asked with a smile. She was checking her camera for film and cleaning the extra lens she carried for distance shots.

"Yes, I guess I'd better get a move on, and I sure could use a strong cup of coffee."

We were members of a tour group of fourteen persons from Arizona "doing" the photo safari sojourn in Africa. My luck gave me a roommate with whom I felt compatible. She was forbearing of my early morning lethargy and I appreciated her unrelenting good cheer.

Our accommodations in the Amboseli Game Park were excellent. Breakfast waited for us in the common dining room after I enjoyed a hot shower in our bungalow. As I stepped under the spray I heard Cheryl call out, "Janet, I'll meet you after breakfast at the Land Rover, okay?" She didn't wait for my response.

Breakfast presented a banquet of fresh fruits, pastries and rolls, hard boiled eggs, dry cereals, milk and cream, English tea and wonderfully rich Kenyan coffee. Knowing the day's outing was to extend well past lunch time, I tucked banana and two oranges, along with a bottle of water, into my new Kenyan woven-sisal tote bag.

The group clustered around the vehicles in the parking area. A tribe (or is it a *gaggle?*) of monkeys scampered about, snatching bits of fruit from each other and watching for any tidbit's the humans might share.

Three Land Rovers with native drivers waited for us. The first two in line took five passengers each. Cheryl and I climbed into the remaining vehicle along with Jeffrey Soames, a retired accountant from Phoenix, and

"Silly Millie," a nervous little woman with a distracted air about her and high pitched voice that put me in mind of a peacock's screech. She was former librarian for the state government archives and looked like she might have spent too many years among the dry tomes. She persistently asked inane questions taxing the driver-guides' command of English—that earned her the name Cheryl dubbed her, though her Christian name was Mildred Wheeler.

Our driver was a handsome black man who went by the tourist awarded name of Benson. We learned that most of the staff used English first names but reserved their true African names for the private lives. Benson was affable, patient with his charges, and happily shared his knowledge of his country, the game preserve, and its animals. He told us he had been leading these safaris for nine years, a plum job due to the tips garnered over and above his modest wages.

Having seen many wildebeests, zebras, and impalas the previous day, this outing promised us elephants. The Masai Mara, in which we traveled, was in fact an extension from Tanzania of the great Serengeti Plain. Few regions of the earth are home to so great an assemblage of awesome wildlife.

Jeffrey and Silly Millie took the seats behind Benson with Cheryl and I in the rear. The overhead opening allowed us to stand two at a time to have clear views of the animals we encountered and to take unobstructed pictures.

The drivers took off by turns, allowing a little distance between vehicles. As we moved out onto the Masai Mara we could still see the leaders but were not so close as to intimidate the animals. Benson slowed down and turned his head to us, "Hush," he said, "look carefully at the hummock of brown grass to the right. A cheetah is there with three cubs. It will be hard for her to raise so many to maturity. They look to be about two months old now." Of course we all wanted to get the best view for our cameras, but we yielded to our two seniors for the first chance.

Mildred let out a squeal of delight and Benson again shed her. "Oh, I'm sorry," she offered, in something between a whisper and a screech. She reminded me of a certain comedian whose trademark is breathless sort of stifled yell. Silly Millie sat down then and Jeffrey did as well, leaving the port open for Cheryl and me. She was the real photographer and affixed her long lens to capture the image in close detail.

We all smiled as we slowly moved away from the mother cheetah tenderly nursing her cubs. Cheryl cried, "Wasn't that wonderful! I think I got some really great shots." Looking beyond, the two other Land Rovers were no longer in sight.

"Benson, where are the other people? I don't see them anymore."

He called back to me, "I believe they have gone beyond that copse near the water. The trees obstruct them from us. Not to worry. We follow the same paths."

Our pace was slow as we paused to view other animals on our way. I never tired of the joy of these creatures in their natural setting. I grew up on Johnny Weismuller's Tarzan, but when Hollywood began making films on location in Africa, the likes of *King Solomon's Mines* and *The African Queen*, I was determined to see for myself at least some of this great "dark continent."

We pulled up near the cluster of dense trees just as a large male elephant was running away. Benson looked alarmed but I had no reason to think that the departing pachyderm was not behaving normally. Benson turned off the motor before his anxiety was triggered. Now he looked around us in all directions and in tense hushed tones ordered, "Don't make a sound. There is danger!" The words were scarcely spoken when an enormous trumpeting shattered our silence and the biggest elephant I shall ever see appeared beside us. His gigantic ears were waving like sails on either side of his head and his trunk whipped back and forth with the agitated swaying of his tremendous body. Cheryl emitted a muffled yelp and Benson put his fingers to his mouth to repeat his caution. Seeing the fear on his face sent a tremor through my body unlike anything ever before. Jeffrey looked as if he were frozen in place. Poor Mildred could not restrain the terrified screech that escaped her. It was the last sound she would utter.

The elephant's bellowing again drowned any smaller noise and the next I was aware of was the lurching of the Land Rover hoisted like some toy and thrown violently upside down. The great bull was not done. He charged head down and pushed us further toward the trees. Once more he picked us up and dropped us on the driver side. In the surreal images of the seconds that passed I think I heard Jeffrey give a cry of pain and saw Mildred thrown like a rag doll out of the Rover. There was a silent pause before the monster trumpeted his defiance and, still swaying angrily, he took a step away from the object of his frustration. I saw him through my broken window as I struggled to straighten up. I spotted Mildred's form in his path. She was face down but started to raise her left arm when the behemoth, with an angry snort, placed a giant foot on her back and strode away from his defeated enemies.

My head was swimming. I touched my hand to my forehead and felt a gash that seemed to go up into my hair. I withdrew my blood covered hand. Now I heard groaning from Cheryl. She was crumpled over and I was partially on top of her. I tried to move off and asked, "Are you badly hurt?

"I don't think so," she responded. "You?"

"I don't feel anything broken, but I guess I hit the grab bar 'cause my head's starting to hurt and I'm bleeding."

"Ladies," Jeffrey spoke, "my leg is broken. I don't think I can move."

"Benson," I called out, "are you all right? What are we to do? How do we get out of this? Benson? Benson!" I could hear the panic in my own voice. It had begun to sink in that I had witnessed Mildred's death and we were in a bad state. Benson didn't answer. I assumed he had been knocked unconscious.

I pulled myself up through the broken window, causing additional lacerations. Some part of my brain noted that I felt no pain from the new cuts. No new marauding creatures were in sight. I let myself down to the ground and stumbled around to the front of the vehicle. Benson was slumped against the door, his head in an unnatural angle and sightless eyes staring upward. His neck was broken. A loud agonized moan jarred the quiet. In a curious second of time delay, I realized that the sound came from me. My knees gave way and I crumpled to the dirt like a pair of worn jeans.

Cheryl joined me there a few minutes later. "Benson's dead," she announced dully.

"I know . . . . Mildred is too." I motioned to where her body lay.

"Oh, my God! Silly Millie, I'm so sorry I ever called you that. I'm so sorry I thought unkind things about you. I'm terribly, terribly sorry!" With that, Cheryl burst into tears and deep sobs.

"Ladies, ladies, can you help me? I can't get out of here without help."

We had forgotten about Jeffrey. His dilemma pulled us from our shock and self-pity and forced us to look at our situation. I struggled to my feet, drew in a deep breath and peered at Jeffrey. I said, "I have some Naproxen in my bag. It may relieve some of your pain. I don't think Cheryl and I can lift you out, Jeffrey. I'm afraid of causing you worse injury if we try. Can you sort of rest your legs against the seat and straighten your back on the door? We are going to have to stay here until someone comes looking for us. That may not be until nearly dark. The other drivers don't know that we had trouble. They probably won't come for us until we're due to check in."

It was Jeffrey's turn to groan. He did manage to ask, "Is Ms Wheeler all right? What is wrong with Benson?" From his unfortunate position he could only see up through the broken window through which I had crawled. When I informed him of the sad fate of our recent friends, he became very quiet and silent tears spilled from his eyes.

I found a broken branch to serve as a hook to reach back into the Rover for my tote bag. The water bottle was intact. I handed it down to Jeffrey together with two of the pain pills wrapped in a tissue.

By this time it was well past one o'clock. I figured we had three to four hours to wait for help.

Cheryl said, "What should we do about poor Mildred? We can't just leave her lying there. This is Africa. By five o'clock there might be nothing left of her to carry back."

That awful thought never crossed my mind, but Cheryl's naturalist training made her the expert. "All we can do is carry her and place her on the Rover and hope we can ward off the hyenas, vultures, ants and whatever, until help comes."

Mildred was a light burden. It was not hard to lift her and put her in place, but the emotional weight didn't leave after her tragic crushed body rested.

Although we were at a high elevation, over six thousand feet, it was July and this was equatorial Africa. The afternoon was very warm. We were only a few feet from water so I risked crocodiles and snakes to go wash the blood from my face and hands. The gash on my forehead stopped bleeding soon after the event, but the blood was attracting flies. A dik-dik, startled by my noisy proximity to his shrubbery cover, darted into other bushes. I actually felt reassured by his presence because this tiny gazelle is a tasty meal for hungry predators and would not be hanging around if they were. Gratefully, no fearsome animals challenged me and I sensibly didn't linger by the water. My ablutions were unremarkable except to remind me of my thirst.

Cheryl and I took turns checking on Jeffrey. He was bucking up very well; I was impressed by his fortitude. I finally asked him if he could spare us each a swallow of water. He had been parsimonious with it and gladly offer it back. I used my stick hook to reclaim it for a welcome swallow. After lowering the bottle back to Jeffrey, I remembered the oranges in my tote. Cheryl and I made short work of these as we leaned against the overturned chassis. I offered Jeffrey the more easily managed banana.

A long three hours passed without anything significant happening, though every sound sharpened our senses. Groups of Thompson's gazelles, larger impalas, and zebra grazed at a distance. Watching the placid animals helped keep my thoughts from the horror I witnessed this day. Cheryl rescued her camera with the help of my stick and took picture after picture, including the grim views of our destroyed Land Rover and our lamented late friends.

Our greatest fear was the possible return of our elephant nemesis. Cheryl speculated that he was pursuing a cow elephant in estrus when another bachelor had the same intention. The females are only available once in two years so are ardently wooed. Our destroyer was evidently running off the usurper when our vehicle suddenly took his place. "Chances are both he and she are miles away by now," Cheryl asserted. It was small consolation to Mildred, Benson, and Jeffrey.

Lengthening shadows gave me pause. I looked at my watch, "It's nearly five," I muttered.

Cheryl asked, "What did you say?"

I said, "Do we have the means to make a fire? I've seen all those movies. You're supposed to build a fire to keep the night predators away. I don't have single match, do you?"

"No, but maybe Jeffrey is a smoker, I'll ask him." She leaned over the Rover. He was asleep, nature was helping him cope with the pain. "Well," she said, "I'll bet Benson would have matches in the glove compartment."

"And how do you propose to get to them?"

"I'll climb through the windshield. We climbed out, didn't we?"

She prepared to do just that when we heard a new rumbling sound. We held our breath as we faced the direction of it. Trees and bushes obscured the way but dust was drifting upward and finally we spotted auto lights.

"Thank you, Lord!" Cheryl exclaimed. "We aren't going to feed the cats and hyenas tonight."

Our rescuers came in two vehicles. A nurse was with them and took charge of getting Jeffrey safely out of the wreckage. Mildred was respectfully wrapped in a blanket and placed on the second seat of a Rover. Benson, too, was lifted by his tearful fellow drivers and gently wrapped in a red blanket. I wondered if there was some significance to their use of that color. I had learned it was the tribal color of the Masai, but Benson had not identified his ethnicity to us.

We were brought back to the Amboseli camp as darkness fell. The camp doctor took care of Jeffrey first. He would be driven to Nairobi early the next morning. The doctor gave his attention to my head wound and decided a few stitches were indicated. I had a double shot of Scotch whiskey before he got his needle out. Of course, this was not the dark ages—he did have Novocaine in his black bag, but I felt I had earned the libation as well.

He questioned me about any symptoms I had during the hours we waited for rescue, and shined a light in my eyes. How could I tell him about the awful trauma that kept repeating in my head; a huge elephant foot coming down on a frail figure in the grass? Instead, I insisted I was fine and just needed a good night's rest. Still not fully satisfied to pronounce me sound, he continued his examination of the minor cuts and emerging blue bruises on various parts of my anatomy. The antiseptic he used stung, but he assured me it would destroy any plague-carrying microbes. Finally he ordered that if I felt dizziness, nausea, or other maladies in the night, I was to report o him immediately. I thanked him for is concern, although I was certain that if I were at risk, such problems would already be manifest.

He gave Cheryl a thorough check as well. She acknowledged bruising in places she didn't know could be bruised. He prescribed two acetaminophen tablets and a good night's rest. Following my lead, she supplemented these with a double shot of Dewars. By the time we put our tired bodies into our beds, we were feeling no pain.

I was almost asleep when a hard wrap on the door roused me. It was our tour leader, Hazel Norwood.

"You ladies have survived a tourist's worse nightmare. Have you had it with Africa? Do you want to return to Nairobi with Jeffrey?"

We looked at each other quizzically and smiled. Cheryl answered for both of us. "The rest of the trip has to be like our desert after a thunderstorm, a wonderful sense of relief. I don't think anything short of a Mau-Mau uprising can compare to *this* day. I'm ready for whatever surprises await us.

The next morning we said "Goodbye" to Jeffrey and promised to send him photos. Before breakfast our fellow tourists observed a brief time of silent prayer for Mildred and took up collection for Benson's family. This was presented to the Amboseli park manager with our condolences.

As we boarded the bus to our new destination, I was sure I heard the distant trumpeting of an elephant. A sudden cold shiver swept over me.

Mary

WHY

My friends kept asking me,—why,
Should I abandon California sky,
Pacific Ocean, Monterey,
Where summers are not warm

But cool and grey, I said:
"I like the mountain peaks
All covered with the snow,
The howling wind,

That makes me feel berserk,
And rain, that gently falls
Upon the earth;
But most of all, I said, I like

The colors of the Arizona sky,
All bright and bold, and as I look,
I see the hand above,
Of Master—Painter in disguise."

Lana

BACK HOME ON THE RANGE

I have finally returned to Wyoming after a temporary lapse of good sense. The last three years of this hiatus in my sanity were spent in Southern California. The lure of surf, skin and nearly perpetual sunshine is grossly overrated. The tension of daily commutes in frenetic traffic, increasing distrust and suspicion, and people, people everywhere, soon became a Velcro straitjacket.

The pressure had increased so insidiously I wasn't fully conscious of it until a relatively minor even caused a jarring shift, much like one of the frequent earthquake tremors. At that moment, my tension was so great I felt as if a person's touch would make me vibrate like a plucked guitar string. I silently screamed, "Get me out of here!"

Within three weeks I had quit my job, packed my little car, arranged for a place to hang my hat at my destination, and was on my way—back to real civilization and mental well being.

As the miles ticked over on the odometer, I could feel the Velcro around my spirit gradually loosening. Ri-i-p.

Along one stretch of road with bluffs high on one side and sloping desert on the other, I saw a yellow diamond road sign reading, "Caution. Eagle Crossing." At twelve and one o'clock above the sign, two eagles were hang-gliding on the updrafts. Ri-i-ip!

Sunlight picked out the fir tops of snowy peaks on both sides of the road. I had not seen another vehicle for many miles and the air was so still I could hear the river racing beside me. Ri-i-p.

I laughed like a madwoman when it began to snow. *Real* weather! Ri-i-ip.

Entering Wyoming was like passing through a culture warp. The first evidence of the crossover came as a gas station attendant warned me to drive cautiously.

"We want you as a customer another day," he said. I looked around to see if he was talking to someone else. Ri-i-p.

My first official act of re-establishing Wyoming as my home was to shed my California license plates. I still feel astonishment when I remember the friendly interest of the police officer who inspected my car and the county clerks who issued my new plates.

The day I finally kicked aside the strait jacket was the day I bumped into an old friend I hadn't seen in 12 years and we picked up where we had left off.

My friends and acquaintances are beginning to roll their eyes at my rhapsodizing over the comparison of the two cultures; the delight of discovery hasn't worn off yet.

Clerks in stores don't demand identification when I write a check. Bank employees don't demand a security deposit for all transactions. Passing strangers smile at me. A grocery checker compares notes with me on a new product. A clothing salesperson, noticing my bookstore package, asks if I've found a good book. Drivers of other vehicles wave as they meet me on the road, and I have yet to hear a plastic, "Have a nice day."

I sit here on my open-air perch above the Platte River and enjoy an autumn mist without being acid-etched. I see an uncluttered horizon and a true-blue sky while I watch hawks, eagles and pelicans soar over the river. I hear the whisper of a rainstorm approaching and know birds will announce its passing. The dog brings me a trophy—a shed antelope horn.

Here in my Wyoming home place, deer and antelope in the driveway are an everyday occurrence; a deer favored us by delivering twin fawns on the grounds of my new workplace. A fox has taken up residence in the culvert up the hill from the house.

If you pass a woman wearing a silly grin, it is probably me still reveling in being back home on the range, breathing air I can't see and feeling free of the binds that tie humans into Velcro straitjackets.

JoLynne

THE MASS MIGRATION

Through the borders from east to west,
From north and south, but mostly southwest,
They are pouring in by the thousands each day,
By foot, by cars, by trucks or vans, and even train, one way.

They see America as the land of the free,
Hoping to have a better life from that which they flee.
Some come legally, but many do not,
Causing numerous problems as we all can see.

Numerous who are caught, are usually sent back,
But many find ways to return again through a different track.
If injured or sick, or lost, or when some never make it,
Directly or indirectly, all suffer and all surely pay for it.

Most people are good and are willing to work,
But there are always some with selfish objectives.
As humans, we all have some rights, but they come with responsibilities,
To honor, respect each other, each country, and have accountability.

Many people are sympathetic to their situation,
But something must be done to end this clandestine "invasion."
Surely, there can come about an acceptable resolution,
Perhaps only greater wisdom and Divine Power will bring about
A reasonable solution.

Loretta

ROAD TO THE PAST

Would you like to walk back to your past,
To correct mistakes?
How many times, with a hasty word, you've caused pain
To a loved one?
How foolish you were to be cross with your Mother,
Just because she wished you well . . .

Wouldn't you like to take your car
And drive back into your past?
To wipe the tears you have caused to those
Who adored you so much!

How many people you could make happier
Just offering a smile instead of a frown.
Even a stranger that met your stare,
Perhaps needed a gentle, comforting glance
To fill his day with some joy.

Oh, how much I would like to return to my past
But the road to the past is gone!

Tatiana

MY HOUSE

I like the house I live in,
It's elevated, on the hill,
But most of all I like
What is within:

Memorabilia and pictures on the wall
Each has the meaning, dating back
Some fifteen years, as I recall,

I would not change, or trade, or sell,
A single item that's in there,
For no amount of cash
If offered,—even in despair!

Lana

TUCSON MAIL TRAIN

Sober Christian gentleman seeks young healthy Protestant lady free to relocate to prosperous ranch near Tucson, Arizona Territory for the purpose of marriage. The lady must have necessary domestic skills and be able to read, write, do accurate sums and have no unseemly vices.

Respond to:Samuel Bartlett, General Delivery
Hotel Congress, Tucson,
Arizona Territory

Samuel read the advertisement for the fifteenth time. The copy carefully sealed in the envelope in his shirt pocket was addressed to the "Classified Column, Chicago Daily News." He had consulted Truett Parnell, the editor and publisher of Tucson's weekly newspaper to learn where to send it.

Sam had been embarrassed to approach Truett with his problem, but after Corabeth Hale declared her acceptance of Josiah Parker's proposal, the number of eligible ladies in a hundred mile radius was limited to the dark-eyed Spanish speaking señoritas. Sam was not unaware of their charms, however, his strict Baptist upbringing would not permit him to consider the devoutly Catholic population of winsome females as candidates for marriage.

Truett had been busy setting type when Sam summoned his nerve and opened the door. A bell jangled as he did so. Truett had installed the device to alert him to visitors over the noise of his printing press when he was in production. He looked up at the sound.

"Good afternoon, Sam. What can I do for you? Do you have a bit of news for me? The paper's going to be kind of lean this week."

Sam moved up to the small counter that separated the reception space from the printing equipment and set his hat on the shellacked boards.

"It's another scorcher today but that's sure no news to print." Saying this, he took a large red handkerchief from his pocket and wiped sweat from his forehead, pushing back unruly russet forelocks as he did so. He put the handkerchief back in its place and nervously smoothed his wiry mustache.

"Well, uh," he stammered, "I, uh, well, I thought you might be the person who could, uh, tell me how to go about something."

"Sam, I've never known you to be at a loss for solving just about any problem, nor have I ever seen you struggle for words. Just spit it out. I'll help if I can."

"The truth is, Truett, I want a woman. No, dang it, that didn't come out right. I want to do this respectable. I want to find a good woman to marry and they're mighty scarce around these parts. I've heard that over there in Bisbee those miners are getting mail order brides. Like there might be someplace back east where you can send off and order them. Do you know anything about how to do that?"

Truett burst out laughing as he exclaimed, "Now don't that just fry your bacon!"

"I'm serious. This isn't funny. If you're just going to laugh at me I guess I'm talking to the wrong person. I thought you were my friend."

"I'm sorry, Sam. It just struck my funnybone to think how you might order up a wife like I order up a supply of printing paper. Those Bisbee miners are putting advertisements in the newspapers back east, in New York and Philadelphia and Chicago. When the ladies answer back they exchange letters and then they decide if they want to pay a lady's fare to travel all the way west to marry a stranger."

"Well, that's what I want to do. How do I start?"

"You start by writing your ad and deciding where you want it published. Keep your ad simple, just include the most essential information. If you get a response you can fill in the particulars in later letters."

"You say some put theirs in newspapers in Chicago? A girl wouldn't have so far to travel from there as she would from those other places. That's probably where I should send the advertisement."

Truett nodded, "I guess that makes sense. Do you have some other things to do while you're in town? I should be finished here around four o'clock. If you'd like me to go over it with you, come on back. You can write your ad here and post it before you head back to the ranch."

"Thanks. Thanks for the offer. I'll be grateful for your thoughts. I don't do much writing."

"Then I'll see you around four."

Sam put on his hat and reached for the door handle. "Right. Four it is."

As he went about gathering supplies, watering his horse, and having lunch at the Mexican cantina on Church Street, he tried to sort out what he considered to be "essential information." By the time he returned to the newspaper office he was pretty sure of what he wanted included. He just needed Truett to help arrange it for an ad.

With the original in his pocket and the copy in its envelope he made his way to the new Hotel Congress across from the train station. Now that the Southern Pacific made a regular stop in Tucson the mail was dropped off at the station and distributed from a special mail window set off from the hotel's reception desk. Sam was assured by Horace Newman that his missive would go out in the next day's mail. Horace was a little officious man who served the reception desk and doubled as Postmaster. One would have thought he owned the establishment by his air of proprietorship, but when one of the Jacomé or Drachman families came in he became treacly obsequious. His saving grace was superb efficiency, so many, including Sam, overlooked his disdainful manner.

Sam routinely came in to town on his buckboard twice a month. He checked for mail on his next regular trip but was not surprised to find none. However, he resolved to check again a week later. This time there were two pieces of mail. One was a bill from the Chicago paper saying if he wanted to run his advertisement a second month he must send them another three dollars. The second piece of mail was clearly in the delicate script of a lady of refinement. Not wanting Horace peering at him while he read, Sam carried the unopened letter back with him to the Church Street cantina where he took a tiny table in the corner and ordered a *limonada*. He carefully opened the envelope and read:

Dear Mr. Bartlett,

I find myself stressed to know how to properly address you or how to respond to your advertisement. I've had no experience of such correspondence, but circumstances press me to take adventuresome steps that I might not otherwise consider.

As to your specifications, I am a Christian of Methodist persuasion. As you may judge, I do read and write. My late parents were educated beyond primary school and insisted that I too be educated. They died of fever when I was but twelve years old. I was sent to live with an elderly widowed aunt in this city. I did her housekeeping and all domestic chores until she too passed from this life early in this year.

From the foregoing you may deduce that I have no encumbrances. I have modest savings from the sale of my aunt's home, as I was her only surviving relative. I am now twenty-six years old. I am told that I am not uncomely, though I am burdened with unruly hair of a dark reddish hue. I am of average stature and generally fit. I am accustomed to hard work. However, the operations of a ranch are unknown to me.

I make it a rule to refrain from the use of elixirs and nostrums of dubious recipe. I will not abide the indulgence of strong drink nor noxious cigars. Another scourge to civility is the use of laudanum or morphine. Our city woefully sees the sad state of aging veterans of the great civil conflict who rely on such substances to see them through their days. They are a grief to their poverty-stricken families.

I trust these particular views of mine are not off-putting in your consideration. I will hope to have your letter of response at your earliest convenience.

Please enlarge on your pattern of life and your personal preferences so that we may each have a clearer basis for determining if our fortunes are meant to meet.

With most sincere regards,
Miss Penelope Anne Morrow
1747 Lake Street, Chicago, Illinois

Sam was ecstatic. He reread the letter three times before carefully refolding it into its envelope. That evening, by his kerosene lamp, he wrote his reply:

Dear Miss Morrow,

My delight is beyond measure. I cannot hope to return a letter that reflects the gentility such as I detect in yours. There is certainly nothing off-putting in your views. They are sensible and morally admirable.

For my part, I am a man of simple tastes and habits. I read portions of the Bible before retiring each evening. I bathe weekly and keep myself clean-shaven except for my mustache. I have all my teeth. I am thirty-one years old and have never married. I am considered a tall man as I stand six feet in my boots. I have some difficulty sustaining a good working weight but I attribute that to my poor skills in cooking for myself. I too have unruly hair that I think of as brick brown. It tends to curl and become bushy.

My ranch is of modest size in these parts, only 2000 acres. My father sold his holdings in St. Joseph, Missouri before the war of the states to pioneer out here. I'm told my mother was a great beauty but of delicate health. She succumbed at my birth. My father's sister reared me to sixteen, when she married a fellow rancher, a widower. Their ranch is in Avra Valley Arivaca, an area north of Tucson. My land is bordered on its west side by the Santa Cruz River and is south of Tucson. I have two Mexican cowboys, they're called "vaqueros," to help me with the cattle. They have a bunkhouse near the main house, which my father built. He's gone now. He was thrown from a horse and a broken rib punctured his lung. He was sixty-nine when that happened.

The house could use a woman's hand. I assure you, you would have free rein to do whatever you would like to make it comfortable for you.

I am Baptist, but I suspect it would not be too hard a stretch to yoke with a Methodist. As we have a circuit preacher, our services are only once a month.

Having been raised an only child, I have always imagined having a large family when I married. Please let me know your thoughts on this matter.

Here in midsummer we are in the hottest days of our desert clime. It begins to cool somewhat in September. If you find my information acceptable, might I hope to plan your travel for the first of September?

With great anticipation,
Your Servant,
Samuel Bartlett

Three weeks passed and again Sam made an extra trip to town to check the mail.

This time the salutation read:

My Dear Mr. Bartlett,

I find myself awed by the size of your ranch. Here in Illinois that would represent four or more farms. How can you possible keep count of your cattle over such a vast area?

I have given much thought to your query about family size. I find myself blushing to think of this as it is immodest for a respectable young lady to speak of such things before a betrothal. Nevertheless, it is a matter of importance and we must know each other well enough to make a sound decision. I can say this, while I am at an advanced age to begin a family, I have often thought it would be good to have more than one child. Life is fraught with hazards. I'm told that Queen Victoria had many children to assure that she would have an heir survive to maturity. I can agree to two, possibly three children. Would that be acceptable to you?

Do you enjoy music? My aunt taught me to play her spinet. I kept it when I sold her furnishings. It would give me much satisfaction if I could bring it with me in September. I have not many other belongings of significance, just a few family portraits and an heirloom spread crocheted by my mother. Other than the spinet, I believe everything could be contained in two trunks and a travel bag.

I am presently living in a hotel for ladies in mid-Chicago. Such things as I have are in the hotel's basement storage. They require only a week's notice for moving.

If you are confident of such a decision, I await travel arrangements.

With growing admiration,
Sincerely,
Penelope Morrow

Sam couldn't contain his bubbling enthusiasm. He burst through Truett's door waving the letter.

"She's coming! She's ready to have my children! She wants me to make the travel arrangements!"

"Whoa, Sam. I didn't even know you'd had an answer to your ad. How come you haven't said anything sooner?"

"Tru, I was afraid if I told anybody I'd jinx it. She sounds too good to believe and she is willing to come all that way to marry me. Isn't that just a knee cracker? Will you be my best man? Who can we get to stand up with her? Do you think Corabeth might? I know she's in a family way but I don't think it's due until December or January."

"Slow down, Sam. I'll be honored to be your best man, but you don't have to marry her the day she arrives. She can stay in the hotel until she rests up and can help plan the wedding. You haven't even told me her name."

"Her name is Penelope, Penelope Anne. Isn't that beautiful?"

"Sam, you sound just like a man who's in love, and you haven't even met her. Amazing."

"Oh, but I will, Truett, I sure will."

Sam went from the newspaper office to the train station. The station agent was getting ready to leave for the day since the train west had gone and the eastbound wouldn't be through until morning. He was annoyed at Sam's insistence that he go back inside and sell him a ticket. After Sam explained that he wasn't going anywhere but he needed the ticket for someone to come there, the agent, grumbling, took out his fare schedule.

"Be sure to include the cost of shipping two trunks, a bag, and a spinet."

The agent grumped, "A spinet, what's that?"

"You know, it's kind of a thing to play music on, sort of like a church organ or a little piano."

"Well that's probably going to cost you like it was two more trunks. You sure you want to do that?"

"Yes, Sir. I certainly do. And there mustn't be a time limit on the ticket. I don't know exactly what day she'll want to travel."

In spite of the agent's grousing, Sam left with the ticket firmly in hand. Crossing over to the Hotel Congress, he importuned Horace Newman for a sheet of stationery and an envelope. Claiming a seat in the lobby, Sam quickly set down his expectations for Penelope's arrival:

My Dear Miss Penelope,

> *It shall be my earnest delight to greet you in person. Enclosed herein is the railway ticket to include shipping charges for your trunks, traveling bag, and spinet.*

As soon as I know the precise day of your arrival I shall reserve accommodations for you at the Hotel Congress so that you may refresh yourself. We can then, at our leisure and your convenience, plan our nuptials.

I am your devoted servant,
Samuel Bartlett

Sam posted the letter with Horace before taking his leave. He found himself singing on his way back to the ranch, "In the sweet by and by, we shall meet on that beautiful shore." He really didn't have any love songs in his repertoire.

A reply awaited him just a week later. His hopeful eagerness had prompted him to make the extra trip to town.

My Dearest Mr. Bartlett,

I am at sixes and sevens to prepare for travel. Being in receipt of the railway ticket, I have given notice of my intention to vacate my residence and have made arrangement for the crating and transport of my spinet and trunks. It remains to place my worldly belongings in the trunks.

You are most thoughtful to offer the respite of a hotel room on my arrival. I anticipate that the travel may prove fatiguing. I shall be buoyed by the joyful expectation of confirming the favorable opinion I have formed from your letters. Barring unforeseen delay, I shall arrive September second.

Your true admirer,
Penelope

Sam washed and ironed his Sunday shirt and brushed his suit. He hung the suit from the porch rafter to let the fresh air clear some of the mothball smell from the fabric. He broke his routine of bathing on Saturday night. Since Penelope was due to arrive on a Wednesday, Sam filled the tub Tuesday evening. He even washed his hair and rinsed it with vinegar water to relieve the tangles. Buttoning his collar and putting on his string tie he thought, I'll just have to do this all over again on my wedding day. But I'm sure it will be worth it.

He was waiting in his buckboard by the station an hour before the train was due. Its arrival time was not always reliable. Its whistle announced it many minutes before it actually steamed to a halt by the small station platform.

In his excitement Sam discovered he was having trouble breathing. He forced himself to take a deep breath.

Two men stepped onto the platform and reached back to unload their respective travel bags. The station agent was handed down the mailbag. Three crates of assorted supplies were set off from the baggage car. The engineer waved an *All clear* to the agent and pushed the throttle forward. The train began to move.

Sam's stunned perplexity kept him silent for the first moment or two. Then, in a panic he yelled, "Wait! Wait! Penelope! Penelope has to get off! Where's Penelope?"

The engineer glanced back and waved as the locomotive picked up speed.

The reality penetrated Sam's confusion. Penelope was not aboard this train. His thoughts were racing. She's been delayed. She'll be here tomorrow. I'll just have to wait till tomorrow.

He checked himself into the hotel and then took his horse and buckboard to the livery stable. He was embarrassed to tell Truett the situation so he avoided the newspaper office. After an early meal at the cantina, he walked back to the hotel. In his room he took off his suit and shirt, hanging them carefully. Stripped to his underclothes, he stretched out on the bed with the breeze from the window bringing some early evening coolness.

He woke at his usual dawn hour and faced a long idle day before the afternoon train was due. At the general store he bought a penny dreadful and carried it back to the hotel lobby where he took a seat out of Horace's immediate scrutiny and settled down to read. That filled a few hours. Leaving the book on a lobby table, Sam made his way to the barbershop for a shave. This was an uncharacteristic indulgence but he had not been prepared to be in town overnight so he had not carried his own razor. Figuring to get his money's worth, he directed the barber to cut his hair as well.

Finally it was time. The whistle again declared the train's arrival. Again Sam waited with the buckboard. This time no one at all got off the train, only mail and cartons of supplies.

Sam felt as if he had been kicked in the stomach. He hadn't had such an urge to cry since he was six years old. He started to turn the buckboard around when the station agent called out, "Hey there, Mr. Bartlett. You have a telegram."

He tethered his horse and went in to the station. He was handed a single sheet of yellow paper. It was addressed to:

> Mr. Samuel Bartlett
> Plans changed. Will explain. Letter follows.
> P.A.Morrow-Wasserman

She must have gotten cold feet, he thought. I just don't understand. What or who is Wasserman?

He tried to figure out how long he should wait for the letter. He decided to come back into town on Saturday.

Horace, who had observed Sam's fruitless vigils, assumed a pompous attitude when he inquired about mail that Saturday and made a great show of sorting through the General Delivery before handing Sam the letter.

Dear Mr. Bartlett,

> *I am obliged to you for the honor you have paid me by proposing marriage. When I boarded the train in Chicago it was my true intent to fulfill our agreement. I had no other plan nor inclination.*
>
> *To my surprise my seat companion was a young gentleman of amiable character. As we undertook acquaintance we found ourselves to be extraordinarily compatible. He explained that he had been in Chicago on a buying trip for his mercantile business in Santa Fe and was making his return.*
>
> *Not to belabor what you may find to be a painful issue, I became convinced that good fortune had destined me for this meeting rather than one in Tucson.*
>
> *Beseeching me to accept his suit, I agreed to terminate my travel at Santa Fe and accompany the gentleman to meet his family. We married the following day.*
>
> *Please be glad for me. Were it not for your kindness and generosity I would not now be a happy bride.*
>
> *I will send you a bank draft for the railway fare. The spinet arrived in excellent condition.*

> *With sincere appreciation,*
> *Mrs. Carl Wasserman*

Sam was shaking his head in consternation. So that's how it is, he thought. This bride by mail is so that I can provide some other fellow with someone to share his bed. If that don't beat all.

Feeling the need to vent his frustration, Sam headed to the newspaper office. As the bell jangled over his head he was puzzled to find a blonde young woman sorting copy at the counter.

The lilting quality of her voice was pleasing as she asked; "May I help you, Sir?"

"Well, I was hoping to talk to Mr. Parnell."

"Oh, hi, Sam." Truett stepped from behind the printing press. "What's happening? I thought I'd be seeing you last week and get to meet a certain someone."

Sam hesitated, "No, there was a change of plans." He didn't want to go into details in the presence of the young lady. He simply said, "That didn't work out."

Truett responded, "I'm sorry. Perhaps it's for the best. What do you think?"

"Maybe so."

"Anyway, Sam, I want you to meet my niece, Cordelia Parnell. She's here from Yuma. You know, my older brother, Silas, her father, is the warden for the Territorial Prison there. He thought Cordelia might meet a better class of people here. She's helping me put out the paper until she decides what she really wants to do.

"Cordelia, this is my good friend Samuel Bartlett. His ranch is south of town."

Cordelia smiled and extended her hand to Sam. He was suddenly aware of her intensely blue eyes, her soft mouth, and the firm grip of her small hand.

Truett said, "I'm having a few folks over for dinner tonight so Cordelia can begin to get acquainted. Can you stay in town? I'd sure be happy to have you join us"

Cordelia interjected, "Oh, please do, Mr. Bartlett. I'd like to hear all about your ranch."

Sam was bewildered. His frustration had left him and in its place was a definite sense that "all's right with the world." He managed to say, "It will be my pleasure, Miss Parnell. What time shall I come?"

Mary

DEEP IN MY HEART

A Thinly Fictionalized Episode of World War II

I was a law school student in Poland when WWII hit Europe. At once life changed. Food disappeared, schools closed. My great expectation of being a lawyer was shattered. Six years we lived hungry. Six years we lived in fear.

We were exchanging silver, jewelry, and clothing for food with farmers. One day, on such an occasion, I was walking home with some potatoes, boiled with skins. I had them wrapped in old newspaper to keep them warm. Suddenly I saw a group of POW's herded by Nazi guards. The prisoners looked like walking corpses—pale grey faces with fallen cheeks. They were hungry and exhausted. Their uniforms, so dirty and rotten, were unidentifiable, their footwear tied in rags while some bleeding toes showed.

I swallowed my tears and when a guard looked away I swiftly unwrapped a large potato an threw it to the prisoner closest to me in the last row. He grabbed it, but the guard noticed it. He shot the prisoner in his hand. In terror, I saw blood coloring his hand and the potato, which he still kept fast.

In shock, I started to run, but the guard sent his dog after me. The dog knocked me down, bit me on my back and right arm. I was sprawled on the pavement; then two or three women lifted me. Both of my knees bled, a piece of flesh hung on the right arm below the elbow. Although the shock masked my pain, I shivered. My teeth were rattling without stopping, although it was summer. Someone put a handkerchief between my teeth and told me to bite hard, to stop the motion of my jaws.

Next they led me into someone's apartment, where and elderly man let us in. One woman explained to me that the gentleman was a retired doctor.

I don't remember what he said to me, all I know is he was shaking his head then handed me a small glass and told me to gulp it quickly. As I hesitated a woman said, "Drink. It's medicine."

I gulped it and at once realized, it was just a strong Polish vodka. But it did the job to some extent. It stopped my shivering. Then while I stood he told me to put my left arm around one of the women and put my face against her shoulder while he would fix the flesh that hung on my other arm. He showed me a thin hook-like needle with a thread, and said that he had no pain killer, so I would have to endure the pain and try not to move.

I braced myself and let him sew the flesh on my arm. From pain I clasped the woman, almost hanging on her.

Afterward he wrapped my arm with a piece of cloth. On my bleeding knees and my back he smeared a dark strong iodine, which burned terribly. Now my tears ran in streams. My whole body felt in total pain.

But a woman said to me, "Endure, don't cry. Think of the prisoner that was shot. His pain must be greater than yours and no one is going to help him."

At once my sobs and tears subsided, for feelings of helplessness for the young prisoner and the pains that he suffered, settled sorrow deep in my heart.

I didn't know to what army those prisoners belonged, since at that time only the uniforms of three nations were known to me; Polish, Russian, and German, yet the whole world was involved in this war.

Whoever those prisoners were, to me it was another great shame of that evil war.

Tatiana

SPRING CALLS

The scent of lilacs is almost overwhelming as it wafts in the open window, bringing with it memories of warm spring days, of lying under my grandmother's biggest lilac bush, and the lessons learned in her garden.

With new grass under me, I can look up through the purple bloom clusters and tiny new leaves to see puffy white clouds drifting, changing shapes from castles to bunnies to cars to whatever my imagination can conjure at the moment. Being still allows me to see things busyness hides.

Early butterflies stop by to savor the aroma before checking out the iris, or "flags" as my Grandma calls them. Purple, yellow, wine, russet, and white blossoms are sprinkled all along the edge of her garden. She doesn't like the rigidity of keeping like colors together in straight, separate rows. She says God wouldn't have given us variety if He wanted everything separate or the same.

The appearance of a ladybug, which doesn't seem to mind me letting it crawl from one hand to the other endlessly, is a harmless celebration of the season. Watching the stop and start flight of a bee, without moving my eyes but by bobbing my head in synchronization, is no longer active enough. I investigate the other lilac bushes forming a hedge around the yard. Several varieties, imported from France, come in shades from white to deepest purple, from single blossoms to ruffled and frilly triple blooms. The laciness of the fancy lilacs intrigue and delight, but the plainer the flower the more intense the scent.

Grandma always expresses dismay when her spade accidentally maims an earthworm. Although I never enjoy picking up worms, she taught me that even the lowly earthworm had a purpose. Breaking up organic matter to enrich and aerate the soil is an important job so we can have more beautiful flowers and delicious vegetables. Planting the tiny plants

Grandma had so patiently started and nurtured from seed in the house encourages gentleness, as we carefully pat them into their new home.

It is a special privilege to remove the straw that blankets the strawberry bed, protecting it from killing frosts. The reward is in spotting the first little berry blossom hidden in the cover, a promise of juicy, sweet fruit to come soon.

Lilacs seem to be indelibly linked in my memory to spirea, the long, whip-like branches loaded with little nosegays of tiny white blossoms. My best friend and I suddenly become fairies, Queen of the May, or at least princesses when we make wreathes for each other from the lopped branches that threaten to block the driveway. Too much of a good thing can become a hindrance.

Pulling the bushel basket of dahlia bulbs out of the crawl space under the back porch is a special spring ritual. It is always exciting to see the sprouting bulbs after their long winter's rest, making the fall chore of digging those bulbs all worthwhile. Some things are more productive after a rest, as Grandma's prize-winning dahlias prove.

All of theses memories came floating in on the intoxicating scent of lilacs, making it impossible for me to stay in bed any longer. I feel propelled to get up and apply the lessons learned, and maybe dig in the dirt a little. Spring calls!

JoLynne

A HOUSE

A house is not a home
Unless it's full of family and friends

It stands all sad and quite alone
And marked with great big corner stone

All kinds of people pass it by
Moms and dads, uncles and aunts

Wandering, why,
That house is always so quiet . . .

No one lives there, people say
Except for spirits of the past

Who gather 'round once a year
Making fuss and knocking down trees

Rumors are, the spirits hunt the house
Because the lives they lived

Were left quite unfulfilled
And some evenings you might

Hear a hollow sound
Of some spirit that cried

For his poor
And abandoned child.

Lana

MY WISH

I wish to be a heron, soaring high, high,
Floating in the air, spreading my snowy-white wings
Against the aqua-marine sky,
And letting the winds take me, wherever they would—
Perhaps to a land where flowers are blooming
With fragrance of lilacs and jasmine,
Where roses are many, many colors!

I wish for the sound of a trickling lovely stream,
Lost among snowy tall mountains.
I wish for the morning sound of a rooster, awakening me
Announcing the time—
At night I wish to dream, while a nightingale sings.

Or perhaps the winds will take me where rivers flow calmly,
Making their way among stones and rocks—with a low tone gurgle,
I wish I were a heron!

Or to the shore of a sea with placid waters
With lazy waves kissing the coast,
With an ever changing design of ivory-lacy foam—

Tatiana

A PETUNIA IN AN ONION PATCH

Eugene, Oregon, home of the Ducks at the University of Oregon, in the beautiful Willamette Valley, and my home. To these ten-year-old eyes, it seemed like the best place to live in the whole wide world. I attended the fourth, fifth, and sixth grade there and had just started junior high school when Dad announced, "We're moving at the end of the month."

Oh, no, not again! I thought. I had just turned twelve and was experiencing my first crush, on a boy who shared my desk in English class. I think he felt a bit of attraction too, though, of course, neither of us spoke of it. My romance was about to end before I had anything to write in a diary.

Moving was a way of life in our family. The house we occupied was, in fact, our fourth residence in the area and by all measures, the best. It was truly a three-story mansion near the university. We didn't own it, of course, only rented, and both Mom and Dad worked two jobs to afford living there.

I was never in a position to be a snob to anyone before, but I loved that big house with its mahogany-paneled dining room, a servant's pantry with a dumb-waiter to the second floor, and two parlors with fireplaces surmounted by broad mantels to show off Dad's treasured ship models. They represented the Nina, Pinta, and Endeavor. Dad cleverly encouraged me to research their history so I would know their significance. The house even had a separate library-study with a large window seat overlooking a great expanse of lawn and huge old maple trees lining the curbs of Broadway, our street. Sometimes, when Mom wasn't home to catch me at it, I slid down the banisters of two flights of stairs. On Saturdays, after all my polishing chores were done, I slipped up to my top floor bedroom to listen to Milton Cross introduce the Metropolitan Opera broadcast on my little Philco radio. There I discovered the world of Bizet, Verde, and Wagner.

But Dad had already accepted the job that required us to move from civilization to the wilds of the Cascade Mountains and a logging community called Culp Creek. Dad was employed by the Oregon, Pacific, and Eastern Railroad (commonly known as the "OP&E") to be their Roadmaster. The line ran from the Bohemia Gold Mine in the high Cascades, by the large sawmill at Culp Creek, and to the Weyerhauser lumber operation at Cottage Grove, twenty-two miles south of Eugene. The employment benefits included a company house rent-free.

So—we moved to Culp Creek and the little house by the railroad tracks. I stared at it in glum resignation. Maybe it had once been painted but there was little evidence now, just grey, weather-beaten wood siding. Mom looked at it with dismay as she said, "Oh, it's going to need a lot of work, isn't it?"

Dad's predecessor was an elderly bachelor. He used one of the two bedrooms (mine) for his woodshed, with a chopping block in the middle and ax marks on the 2x6 plank wood flooring. The kitchen held a single sink, vintage 1900, and a cold water spigot protruding from the wall. Adjacent to this a pair of stacked packing crates served as counter space. The pot-bellied stove in the living room supplied heat. The old man had constructed a sandbox around the stove in a rectangle about 2 ½ ft. by 4ft. This had the dual purpose of fire safety and an area for drying kitchen refuse that he would later burn in the stove. There was no garbage service so whatever accumulated was burned or buried. "Don't even think about a bathroom," I told myself. The outhouse was a one-holer set slightly uphill and a bit north of the residence, promising a brisk walk in winter.

The place wasn't entirely primitive. We had electricity.

The three of us wrestled the chopping block out of the woodshed-cum bedroom, and Dad unloaded some of the biggest boxes from the borrowed truck in which we had moved. Mom unpacked these as quickly as she could and Dad broke down the boxes. I swept out the splinters and shavings from *my* room and Dad spread the flattened corrugated cardboard over the floor for insulation. Only then were we able to assemble my bed.

Worn linoleum covered the other bedroom floor. After giving it a good scrub, we put up my parent's bed. My job was to make the beds ready for sleeping.

Mom cleaned out the sandbox and Dad got a cheery fire going in the potbelly. Baloney sandwiches and canned soup was our first Saturday night dinner in our new home.

On Monday Mom went with me to register for the seventh grade at my new school. I prayed it wasn't another one-room school such as the one in which I started first grade. It was, instead, five rooms, with and indoor restroom. Almost uptown. I looked around at the kids gathering before the bell rang. The girls were wearing bluejeans! And several of the boys had suspender coveralls.

I hissed at Mom, "I'm *not* going to wear bluejeans. I'll die first. They look like hillbillies!"

"Hush," she said, "they'll hear you. You'll wear the clothes you have. Now, be still."

I discovered that my teacher was also the principal and taught both seventh and eighth grades in one room. His wife taught three other classes and a two more teachers completed the faculty. My class was the largest, with fourteen students. There were six eighth graders. I soon realized that I was on par with the eighth grade material so my homework was a snap. These kids were not well read and their homes held few books. Their fathers were loggers, sawyers, and lumbermen. They related to what they knew well, the rugged land, and not to literature and scholastic pursuits.

In spite if being the odd newcomer, my classmates received me well, and were impressed by my success with our studies. They soon nicknamed me "Dictionary." They said it with kindness, so I wasn't offended. Clothing styles had nothing to do with social status in their frame of reference, so they were neither impressed nor insulted by my resistance to bluejeans, it just didn't matter.

Meanwhile, Dad tackled the house to make it livable. He scraped the siding and painted it a deep cream color, with shutters at the windows. He laid new heavy linoleum in bright colors on the floors in every room. Mom sewed curtains for the windows that she had cleaned to pristine clarity. Dad built a proper long countertop with drawers and cabinets in the kitchen. He reworked the electrical wiring and thrilled Mom the day he installed a small electric range.

By Christmas I was not ashamed to bring my new friends to our home. After school activities were limited to hiking in the mountains or by the river, and visiting at friends' homes.

Between the railroad tracks and the highway was a huge abandoned loading dock overgrown with blackberry brambles. Berry season was over by the time we moved in, but I could see there would be great pickings the next summer. On the south side of the highway was the Row River (pronounced as "wow"). It was mostly a whitewater river fed by mountain springs and snowmelt. When summer came I learned to swim in that treacherous and icy stream, because that's where the other kids went swimming.

On a Sunday afternoon, before school let out for the summer, I was invited to join the bunch of kids going "sliding." I found out that there might be an advantage to bluejeans after all. The sport involved sliding on one's backside down the slope of the enormous sawdust mountain at the sawmill. My skirt and undies were embedded with itchy sawdust with one ride. In spite of that I went back to the top for another go.

Culp Creek boasted a Weyerhauser company-owned general store. Kids bought candy and ice cream bars there if they had earned any spending money. Weekly allowances for kids hadn't been invented yet. At least two of the boys in my schoolroom thought I was cute enough to volunteer to carry my books home for me. I knew it was getting serious when they invited me to the store for ice cream.

I graduated from the eighth grade at Culp Creek. For the first time ever, the graduates wore rented caps and gowns for the ceremony. That was due to my instigation as Valedictorian of the class. I was invited to play my violin as part of the entertainment, and Dad was asked to do a reading. He read a poem he had long cherished titled "Just Like His Dad." I don't remember what I said in my valedictory address, I'm sure it was some gushy thing about being "launched on the sea of life." The truth was, only a couple of my classmates went on to the nearest high school, in Cottage Grove.

Dad completed the work at Culp Creek for which he had actually been hired, to construct a switching yard for trains by the sawmill. The train to Bohemia Mine ran only twice a week, but the mill required turnaround capabilities every day. Dad's self taught civil engineering skills I still find impressive. He left school in the tenth grade.

One day in late summer he said, "I've rented us a house in Cottage Grove so you won't have a long bus ride to school. You'll be able to walk to school."

"But, Daddy, my friends are all here!"

"Honey, I'm sure you'll make new friends, and I'll be starting a new job."

Once again we loaded up and moved out. I looked around my sunny, pretty bedroom and sighed wistfully. I hoped whoever used it next would appreciate its transformation.

Some of my friends waved goodbye as we passed the general store. I tried not to let Mom and Dad see my tears in leaving behind what I now valued, not an onion patch, but a joyous adventure in a natural garden.

Mary

THE SEA

As I was walking
Along the shore,
The bright blue sky
Was stretching
Forever above,

And the waves
Were splashing
According to rhythm
Being very careful,
Not skipping the beat . . .

And every time
I turned around
I heard the seagulls' cry,
Flapping their wings
In the deep blue sky;

And the tiny crabs
Were playing
Their hide and seek
Right at my feet,
In the sand below.

Lana

THINGS

ECONOMIC BLUES
OF 2008

All of a sudden
There was a chill
The air grew cold
And the time stood still . . .

Is it a calm before a storm
Or just a feeling
Of a predicted gloom
After so many years
Of economic boom?

It's hard to guess . . .
When our nation, in distress,
Is struggling and in pain
Just trying to survive
The biggest economic stress,
That came her way,

Our so-called friends
Are turning their backs
Pretending, they have
Never seen or heard
About the raging storm
That's sweeping our land . . .

Lana

CROCHETING LEPER BANDAGES

Sherrie sat at the library book sale waiting for customers to make a purchase. Meanwhile she crocheted. Sometimes, she would look down at what she was doing. Other times, she would look up and chat with some of the people who stopped by making an inquiry about the book sale. Others stopped to ask what she was making. "Oh" was the reply with a sort of puzzled look when she answered, "I'm crocheting a leper bandage." Several were more curious and had more questions. Sherrie herself knew little about the disease and that it's found in certain areas of the world. She wanted to learn more and found out that she was not alone.

She discovered that those affected had a need for the crochet bandages. This started when her church ward women's organization selected crocheting as a service project. The women all learned that these crochet bandages were softer on the skin than the regular bandages, more durable and were reusable because they could be washed without falling apart like the regular bandages.

The women were happy to become involved in the project. Many had experience in crocheting. But, there were also many with little or no experience at all, and were eager to learn. All were glad that they could do something for someone who had a disease they had limited knowledge of. This would be a project worth undertaking and a great learning experience.

After some planning, preparation, and instructions, it wasn't long before the women got started on the project. Those with experience crocheting made themselves available to the others with little or no experience. Soon there was a network of women setting goals and a deadline for completing the project.

Because two women of the project, Nancy and Diane knew very little about the disease, they decided that along with learning to crochet, they would do some research and would report back to the women the following week. The next few days were busy for both women as they had their families to care for and other activities. But they were excited about what they learned and shared it with not only the other women, but also their family members.

Another name for leprosy is Hansen's Disease. The organism causing the disease, was discovered by a Norwegian physician Dr. A. Hansen (1841-1912). This is a chronic, bacterial infection that damages nerves, mainly in the limbs and facial area. It is systemic, characterized by progressive skin lesions. With timely and correct diagnosis and treatment, the prognosis is good and is rarely fatal. If untreated, it can cause severe disability, unsightly appearances and disfigurement, and blindness. It is not highly contagious.

A person is infectious to others only during the first stages of the disease. People living in prolonged close contact with an infected person are at risk of infection and that only three percent of the population is susceptible to leprosy. Leprosy has a very long incubation period, about three to five years. Most of the destructive effects of the bacteria on the nervous tissue are caused, not by the bacterial growth, but by the reaction of the body's immune system to the organisms as they die. As the disease progresses, the peripheral nerves swell and become tender and hands, feet, and facial skin eventually become numb and muscles become paralyzed.(1) The crochet bandages are used to protect the affected upper and lower extremities and provide comfort also for those affected. The crocheting of bandages started approximately thirty years ago and women throughout the world engage in this service.(2)

In 1992, the World Health Organization estimated that there were 5.5 million cases. Prior to that, from 1960 to the 1980's the estimated number of cases world wide ranged from 10-20 million cases. Leprosy is prevalent in tropical areas such as Africa, Southeast Asia, and South America. In the U. S. most cases occur in Hawaii, and small parts of California, Texas, Louisiana, and Florida. In Hawaii, a leper colony exists on the island of Molokai in an isolated area of the island.(3)

Members of the crocheting group approach it in different ways. Linda thinks this is an ideal project because for her it is relaxing after a busy day and she can do it even while watching television. It also makes her feel good that she is doing a service for someone and not a difficult thing to do. Laura crochets when waiting in a doctor's or dentist's office and also while riding as a passenger in a car. Miki crochets during her part-time job as a nanny when the children are asleep. Sometimes she even does it between classes while in school because it's relaxing.

Laurie now takes her newly learned skill with her whenever she takes her son to baseball practices or games. She was so thrilled when she finished her first bandage.

Julie discovered the value of making these bandages and the joy she found in serving. She got a few of her neighbors, friends, and family members interested and involved also.

A few days after the project was announced at the meeting, Susan started her crocheting after putting her fourteen month old baby down for a nap. It wasn't long before she had completed nearly ten rows when her nine years old daughter, Melanie and six years old Justin came home from school. Susan greeted her children warmly after putting down her crocheting.

"Oh, Mom, what's that you're making? May I see it?" asked Melanie.

"Sure, you may, but would you and Justin like a snack first?" her Mom replied.

"Yes, yes, I do!" shouted Justin.

"OK, I guess I'm a little hungry," said Melanie as they started walking toward the kitchen.

"After your snacks, don't forget to put away your things properly in your rooms where they belong, all right?" instructed their Mom.

"Okie-dokie," the children replied.

"And try to be quiet as your brother is taking a nap," their Mom added, "and don't forget your homework if you have any."

Later that afternoon, Melanie asked her Mom about her crocheting. After explaining the project to both her children, Melanie wanted to learn to crochet and try making a bandage. She thought it looked easy enough.

"May I, Mom?" she asked. "I can do it. I know I can." Justin, of course, was more interested in playing.

"Of course," said her Mom. "But remember, if you start one, you need to complete it," her Mom instructed her. "Someone will be using what you make," she added, "and your Dad will be very happy that you want to get involved and learn a new skill too."

Melanie received her first lesson on crocheting that evening after dinner. It was slow and tedious at first. Melanie had difficulty with the thread getting tangled at first, and it was frustrating. Susan reminded her daughter that it takes time to learn something new and that she was doing fine. Stan watched his daughter and encouraged her not to give up and be patient.

"Remember," he said, "it takes time and practice." After an hour or so at it, Susan informed her daughter that it was almost time to get ready for bed and that she could crochet again tomorrow. Melanie felt relieved as her fingers and hands were getting tired and sore. Justin and baby Rob were also ready for bed.

The next day, after coming home from school, Melanie decided she wanted to help with the project, especially after her teacher talked about how lucky we are in this country. She was going to do it even if it was hard. Her Mom and Dad were happy with her decision and purchased a crochet needle and thread for her. Melanie was glad and promised not to give up. She started that evening with more lessens and practicing.

After two weeks, she almost mastered the simple pattern of the bandage and hardly needed help from her Mom. She had almost completed one bandage and was anxious to start another. This time, she wanted to do it by herself.

The women's group had decided they wanted to complete two hundred fifty bandages to send to the Humanitarian Center in Salt Lake City by the end of two months. There were about twenty-five women involved in the project. Each bandage was approximately five inches wide and three feet long. After seeing some pictures of victims of the diseasee, Melanie decided she would try to complete at least four bandages. She felt so sad when she saw the pictures and felt the need to help. Her Mom was very happy that her daughter felt compassion toward others and wanted to participate.

With school, church, and other activities, she would be quite busy for the next two months trying to accomplish her goals. Even Justin wanted to help and volunteered to do a chore or two.

A few days before the end of the month, Melanie had completed nearly two bandages. Her Mom had just started her fourth bandage. Melanie and her Mom spent every spare minute they could crocheting without sacrificing the other chores and family activities. Justin fed Melanie's cat, Dusty, for her almost every day and he and Rob spent more time together. Rob especially enjoyed the little stories Justin read to him. Both even played with Dusty and had fun with him.

Before the end of the second month, Melanie completed her fourth bandage just before going to bed. She was so happy!

Her Mom had completed almost ten bandages. She had approximately a dozen more rows to crochet and planned to complete them that evening. Rob, however, caught a cold and was very fussy. Justin tried to play with him, but he was not happy with his runny nose and a slight fever of almost a hundred degrees.

Earlier, Dad did the dishes and Melanie and Justin helped clean up the kitchen so Mom could tend to Rob. Besides his cold, Rob was teething. His gums were swollen and he drooled all over. He was not happy at all. Dad had to leave shortly after doing the dishes to attend a meeting. Melanie and Justin went to bed soon after their Dad left.

It was fairly quiet with only the sound of music from the stereo and an occasional whining from Rob. Melanie was tired but not really sleepy yet so she grabbed a book and started to read. Soon, she heard loud crying from Rob and he was being very fussy. She also heard her Mom trying to calm him down. After listening to his whining and crying a short while, she decided to help her Mom out. She snuck out of bed and went to her Mom's room. She found the unfinished bandage and went quietly back into her room and got busy. In the meantime, Mom decided that it was time to give Rob some medication for his pain and fever. It was a bit of a struggle getting him to take it, but he did finally swallow some Tylenol elixer.

Approximately half an hour later, Rob started to settle down and was no longer crying, whining, and being so fussy. But it took a little while longer rocking him before his Mother could put him down. Finally, he went to sleep.

Mom sat down to rest on the couch. She was so tired. She closed her eyes and almost fell asleep when she was startled by the back door opening. She opened her eyes and saw her husband come in.

"Oh no, you're home already?" she said. "What time is it?" she asked.

"Almost ten-thirty," he replied. "Guess Rob kept you busy, huh?"

"Yes, and I haven't been able to finish the bandage. Guess I'll stay up a little while longer," she said.

"Well, you stay here, and I'll go get it for you. Then I'll stay up with you while you finish it. Shouldn't take you long, right?" he said.

"Okay. I think I have about a dozen more rows to do, and it'll be finished," she answered as he walked toward their bedroom.

In a few minutes, he returned. "I thought you said you didn't have a chance to finish it," Stan said, "look what I found," he added as he handed the neatly folded bandage.

"What? Let me see that," said Susan, as she reached out for the bandage. She smiled. "You know, I didn't finish this, but think I know who did."

"Melanie!" they both exclaimed at the same time. "This is wonderful!" Susan smiled.

"You bet," said Stan. "Our daughter is growing up!" he added as he went over and embraced his wife.

The next morning, it was Saturday. Susan took Melanie with her to the meeting along with all the bandages they crocheted. It was a busy morning at the church building. There were more than thirty-five women there plus another ten daughters who also participated crocheting. When all was counted, there were five hundred and two leper bandages completed. The women wrapped and boxed the bandages ready to be sent to the Humanitarian Center to be distributed for those in need. Not only was the gathering a service one, but also a social one. The ladies and girls bonded and got to know each other and enjoyed a pot luck lunch together! How happy the women and girls were, especially Melanie and her Mom!

Loretta

*   *   *

1   The American Medical Association Home Medical Encyclopedia Vol. 2 I-Z Medical Editor-Charles B. Clayman, MD. Published by the Reader's Digest Assoc., Inc. with permission of Random House, Inc. New York. Copyright 1989 by Dorling Kindersley Ltd. and the American Medical Assoc., pgs.634-635.

2   The American Heritage Dictionary of the English Language; William Morris, editor; Published by American Heritage Publishing Co. Inc. and Houghton Mifflin Co. Copyright 1969 by American Heritage, 2nd printing. All rights reserved under Bern & Pan American Copyright Conventions. Manufactured in USA. pg 599 and 749.

3   The American Medical Association Home Medical Encyclodedia, pg. 634.

ASH PINK CURTAINS

We sit on the soft, silk sofa, watching the sunset sky,
Mother and I
Six young kittens have a wild play, running the spacious room,
Sliding on the parquet floor. We laugh—
The breeze is moving ash-pink curtains on a
French open door.
One kitten runs and hangs on the curtain, swaying, having fun,
The others follow the game.
"Oh my dear, oh my!" My Mother's cry, They will ruin the curtains,
Brand new curtains!"
"Don't worry, Mama, kittens, not curtains are important for us."
The years passed by—I sit on the same silk sofa watching
The grey cloudy sky.
Cats . . . gone, Mother too . . .
Two story home silent . . . I sit alone.
The ash-pink curtains still swaying there
Looking like new.

Tatiana

MY PLANT

I have a plant that grows
And seems to be content,
Spreading its branches
All over the place, and yet,
As if asking and begging for help . . .

"You are growing too fast," I say,
"There's no way, I could train
Your branches
That are long and green,
Gently swaying in the wind;

And if I really would cut
All of your branches to the core,
Like people say, I should,
You'd lose your dignity and face
And fall into complete disgrace . . .

Just grow as fast as you would like
And listen only to your own heart,
Enjoy your freedom while you can
And spread your branches
Far and wild!"

Lana

REQUIEM FOR CASSIE

I am wary of people who always insist on explaining how things work. Some things in life just shouldn't be reduced to the lowest possible denominator! Why dim the beauty of a rainbow by focusing on the scientific explanation of sunlight prismed through raindrops on a backdrop of dark cloud? Or of the amazing sight of sundogs reduced to ice particles in the clouds reflecting sunshine? No doubt many of you can explain how my email messages get from here to there. I don't want to know! Mark Twain said we should keep our illusions, because when we give them up, we will survive, but will cease to live.

As I crossed a bridge over the Platte River one day, I spotted a spout of water and was curious about it. It was there again when I crossed the bridge a few weeks later. I laughed to my sister that we had our own Loch Ness monster, even going so far to name it Cassie. Being of a much more analytical mind than I, she discovered the spout was caused by the backflushing of the sewage treatment plant as it emptied into the river. Cassie died in that unglamorous explanation.

I do not feel we are particularly enriched by knowing all the WHYs in our lives. Enjoy details of life simply for the richness they add to your existence. Never cease to be awed and appreciative of rainbows, and leave me my illusions.

I still mourn for Cassie!

JoLynne

OUR TALENTS

The Lord has blessed each of us with talents
For use in our daily lives.
A smile or a gentle word of kindness
Pays dividends far more for one deprived.

Helping hands for service and daily chores,
Some music heard, played, or sung
Can lift spirits of many bearing burdens,
Bringing moments of peace to hearts tightly strung.

Each one of us is gifted in more ways than one,
Others hidden, to be discovered, if we but have the drive.
Some with few, some with many,
Some not easily recognized, but if they are, we will thrive.

All of us need to grow, learn, develop and pursue,
The skills, abilities, and knowledge capable from within.
Through desire, work, study, and persistence,
Our talents bring happiness, peace, and fulfillment.

Loretta

SAFEWAY LUGGAGE

My name is Irma Harrington, at least, that's the name I wound up with.

Growing up in foster care loaded me with a lot of invisible baggage, but one of my earliest memories was staggering up some steps hugging a brown grocery bag containing my stuff. I later came to know these paper bags as "Safeway Luggage," what us foster kids hauled our belongings in from one foster home to the next.

That first memory was when I was around three years old, though I had already been in the system since I was born, and years later tried to piece together the fabric of my life.

By the time I was in the third grade I was in my fourth foster home. That was when they had me tested by the school shrink. The teacher said I seemed to daydream most of the time, but I was the top reader in my class and could already multiply and divide numbers.

Reading and daydreaming made life worth living. Adventure stories and fairy tales were even better than chocolate pudding for dessert.

I read about mountain climbers and imagined my *real* parents died tragically in an avalanche of snow. Or a story about an unhappy princess would lead me into believing I was a baby stolen from the beautiful princess and would one day be discovered by her prince who had been searching for me for many years.

As I grew older my imaginings became more sophisticated. I decided what happened was, I wandered away from the careless nursemaid who was supposed to be watching me. Some hippies found me in the park and carried me away with them. But they were arrested for smoking pot and I was put into a foster home.

There had to be some reason why my birth parents didn't want me. By the fourth foster family I figured out that no one else much wanted me either.

Entering my teens, the scenario I settled on was that my real mother was an unwed pregnant teenager who relinquished me to the adoption agency, but nobody adopted me because my eyes were crossed.

Surgery had corrected that problem when I was in the second grade. Hooray! I could read easily then and books became my life. I ignored teachers, foster parents, and classmates (who all seemed to have at least one parent).

As a result of the psych testing in third grade, I was put into an accelerated academics program. They said I would pay more attention. I did, sort of. The best part was, I was allowed to read at any level I could understand. My interests soon moved beyond children's stories.

High school days were not *Happy Days* for me—not like "The Fonz" and his cohorts. I overheard comments like "nerd," and "the dictionary," and "dull as dishwater." I guess the one that always hurt most was, "Well, you have to feel sorry for her—she's just a foster kid." But this kid had something going for her.

My caseworker (my eighth) set up a meeting for me with the high school principal, the psychologist, my home room teacher, and a representative of the Casey Foundation. I had no idea what it was about or how it would change my life.

The home room teacher referred to my exceptional scores on standardized tests. The shrink said my IQ and aptitude scores were impressive. The case manager said she was recommending me for placement in a Casey home.

My first thought was—*Oh, no. Pack up the Safeway Luggage. Here we go again.*

The Casey rep explained that once I was matched with a Casey family, I could remain with them until I completed my education, and that meant all the way through college if I chose. The foundation would pay my college expenses.

I guess I just sat there stunned with my mouth hanging open. Of course, I wanted college, but foster kids are out on the street when they turn eighteen. I figured college was a hopeless dream for me.

After three interviews I was matched with Darryl and Joyce Harrington.

Darryl was the Patient Advocate for the Veteran's Hospital. Joyce was a judge of the Superior Court. Their only son had just graduated from the university and was on a fellowship for study in England.

They had a beautiful home in the foothills and a library that filled one whole room.

I made it through the university with honors, and earned my Juris Doctorate with a specialization in children's law, that is, dependency and custody laws pertaining to children. I have a career as a practicing attorney and advocate for children's cases.

With the family's permission and encouragement, I legally took the name of Harrington for my own.

After years of backtracking and legal stumbling, I learned my teenage speculation was right on the mark. My teen birth mother relinquished me at birth and had gone on to become a housewife and mother to my three half-siblings. My birth father died of a heart attack about the time I graduated high school. He had been a young airman who was sent overseas without ever knowing he left a pregnant girl behind. I exchange Christmas cards with my birth mother, but my real family is Darryl and Joyce.

Whenever I see a grocery sack from Safeway I remember the day I put my Safeway Luggage in the trash for the last time.

Mary

MY HEART

I took my heart
To the storage today
And there it will stay . . .
Until there's a reason
To claim it again.

I have no use for it
Just now,—it's easier
To live without the heart,
And I truly must say
It just gets in my way . . .

I don't feel sorrow
And I don't feel pain,
No love and no friendship
Are coming my way,

I move and I smile
And I talk a lot,
But no one knows
That I have no heart!

And soon enough
I will become
An empty shell,
But free at last,
Once again!

Lana

BEST BUDDIES

"Look, Maw! Ain't he purty, Maw?"

Only a scruffy, grubby, barefooted ragamuffin in grimy overalls with torn knees would find the emaciated, smelly, matted half-grown Collie mix pup pretty.

"Can I keep him Maw? He likes me and I already taught him a trick. Watch! Lay down, Spike. See, he minded me. Can I keep him, please, Maw?"

The pup had flopped down beside Jake, probably from hunger and weakness, rather than obedience. It would have taken a heart of obsidian for Maw to say no to the earnest pleading of her youngest son who had lost his heart to a cur as gangly as he. The pup had a name already, and it was obvious the family of three boys now had a pet.

Bathed, brushed and fed what seemed like enormous quantities of leftovers and scraps, supplemented with horsemeat from the butcher, Spike was better able to live up to his owner's accolades. Jake took on the job of sweeping out the butcher shop and washing the windows in exchange for the meat scraps that helped Spike fill out. The physical work of moving barrels of bones and trash built muscles that helped Jake fill out too.

Spike was Jake's second self, one not moving without the other, except for time spent in the butcher shop and in school. Spike waited patiently in the shadows outside the back door of the store, napping but instantly alert to the step of his master. During school hours, Spike lay on the merry-go-round the school janitor had built out of scrap metal for the kids. The dog was the hero of every grade school recess, riding the spinning platform until he was whining from dizziness. No matter how disoriented, he would not leave the carousel until his human appeared for lunch or the end of the day. Only by enduring a weekly bath was Spike allowed in the house, and it was an open secret that Spike slept on the bed, sprawled beside Jake, instead of on the rug as decreed by Maw.

Summertime trips to the swimming hole in the river below the defunct power plant became the highlight of the pair's days. Not to be left behind while Jake had fun in the water, Spike taught himself to grab the dangling knotted rope and swing himself out to drop mid-river. Jake and Spike raced each other to the sand bar, which provided the best exit point to run back to the rope swing and do it all over again.

Although the other kids at the swimming hole accepted Spike as one of the gang, he mostly ignored them unless someone got into trouble because of the tricky river current. He pulled more than one of them to safety on the sand bar, earning his place as a prominent and respected member of the community.

Everyone knew where Jake was, Spike would be. The day he came home alone, barking furiously, everyone instantly knew that bad news about Jake was next. Thanks to Spike, Jake quickly got the medical attention he needed after falling though the rotted floor of the power plant. The constant moisture and long-term neglect had made the old red brick building unsafe and off-limits by order of the town council. But what teenage boy can resist a double-dog dare? It took the volunteer fire department two hours to extract Jake from the broken timer and the junk stored in the crawl space. Spike learned to sleep on the bedside rug while Jake was confined amid pillows propping his broken leg. Only the fact that the dog was within ear-scratching reach kept both boy and dog from rebelling.

As they both reached their mid-teens, hunting season became a favorite time of year for Jake and Spike. A buddy was allowed the use of his father's ancient pickup for the pheasant hunting trips. Howard would slow in front to the house, oogah-oogahing without completely stopping, the signal for Jake and Spike to dash out, ready to go. Jake would dive through the glassless window into the seat, followed by Spike who somehow managed to find and keep a toehold on the running board. To everyone's amazement, he seemed to prefer this to riding in the bed of the truck. The old-timers sitting in the sun on a bench outside the bank would shake their heads in bafflement at "that durn dog of the Wade boy."

The talk on the bank corner, in the stores and at the post office became focused on war news. Each week the names of one or two more farm boys were listed on the bulletin board at the post office as enlistees. Occasionally, hushed voices would talk about one of them being 4-F, a hard label to bear. As they each finished high school, Jake's two older brothers enlisted, one in the Army, one going to the Navy. As the youngest and only son at home, Jake was the focus of Maw's prayers for the war to end soon, along with prayers for the safe return of her other two sons. The Army sent Floyd to Ft. Riley, Kansas to work in the motor pool. The Navy put Melvin aboard ship for some unspoken destination in the Pacific. As the war roared on, to the East and the West, Jake impatiently awaited his high school graduation to enlist in the Army. He was caught up in the patriotism and idea of glamour of a uniform, like so many of the boys not-yet men were.

Jake said a choked-up goodbye to Maw and came close to going AWOL at having to say good-bye to Spike. He gave Spike orders to stay out of trouble and to wait for him to come home, not running off to someone else. Spike took the orders to heart and spent his days lying under the rural route mailbox, watching the road for his friend's return. He seemed to know when the mailman delivered letters from forts across the States and finally from France. The only time he left his daytime vigil by the mailbox was to let Maw know one of those letters had arrived.

One day he refused to come to the house at nightfall for his food. He stayed on guard for a whole week, refusing food but drinking the water Maw finally took out to him. He broke his watch; dejectedly letting Maw know the mail had arrived. A Red Cross nurse wrote the letter from a field hospital somewhere in the Netherlands and Maw deciphered between the censor's black marks that Jake had been wounded. He had been transported to the hospital where he was recovering, expecting to be sent home as soon as it could be arranged. The information was scant and spotty, so it was impossible to determine the extent of his wounds.

Spike resumed his daily routine. No letters came and he didn't even lift his head when the Western Union man came. Only Maw received the black-bordered telegram in stunned agony. She sat alone, numbed to mindlessness until dark when her practical nature recalled her to her responsibilities. She mechanically shut the chickens in for the night and then called to Spike, hoping for some comfort from him. When he didn't come, she took food and water to him again, but knew immediately he wouldn't need it. She buried him at the bottom of the garden, telling neighbors he died of a broken heart.

Jake's medals and possessions finally arrived, with a letter explaining the hospital took a direct bomb hit and all perished. The medals were buried next to Spike's grave. The men of the VFW made a marker that read, "Jake Wade and Spike, Best Buddies to the End."

JoLynne

SONG OF THE WESTERN SKY

Oh western sky, oh western sky! Filling, thrilling my heart,
As I watch evening colors until I cry from joy, until I cry,
Ever changing colors from pale blue to brilliant crimson,
Then to orange and red, oh no, no, no, I can't describe,
You must come to see the western sky!

And I watch as the evening slowly dies
The sparkling moon emerges with a riot of brilliant stars
From behind Sierra Vista's mountains, that form a capricious line
Against exaltation of celestial glory!

If you wish to know where angels dwell,
You must see the Arizona sky!
Oh western sky, oh western sky!

Tatiana

A FISH

I am a fish, that one fine day,
Was caught in waters of the bay;
I was too small to eat
A shame—to throw away . . .

The boy has finally decided
To get me off the hook
And after that he threw me back
Into the deep blue bay.

But injuries that I received
From hook that ripped my gill
Have not completely healed
And I am constantly in pain . . .

Somehow I cannot swim as fast
As all my buddies do
And always am left behind
By the rest of the crowd . . .

Lana

THE CLOUDS

Have you ever looked up at the clouds and seen
A cowboy on his horse crossing a stream?
Or a huge snowman with an old squashed hat?
Or even a giant white bear with a baseball bat?

Have you ever glimpsed up and saw in the sky
A speeding race car swiftly going by,
And not too far behind came an odd-looking turtle,
With it's head lifted up and it's shell slightly purple?

And every once in awhile as you look at the clouds
Hundreds of white, fluffy puppy dogs gather like crowds.
Then there are clouds like giant cotton candy
Helping to nourish other experiences so dandy.

At times, blankets of deep gray clouds hang overhead
One just feels like crawling into bed
For it sets a similar mood of gloom for some
And for a few, there seems no brightness that will come.

But soon, a display of lightning precedes loud thunders
Then a downpour of rain or just a few scattered showers
Nature then shifts its course, and the sun will appear
Clouds dissipate, the sky is once more majestic and clear.

Aren't we and our lives like the clouds up above,
Often changing in thoughts and appearances?
Together, apart, in crowds, or alone somewhere,
Each different, unique, not exactly the same anywhere?

It is peaceful and quiet and sometimes so still,
The sky is clear, it is blue, and not a cloud is seen.
How grateful one feels, what a joy, what a thrill
To have glimpses of nature, of God's love, and His being.

Loretta

INNOCENCE LOST

"It's doing it again!" The cold, shiny key winked brazenly at me from its hiding place in the desk drawer. I'd always resisted it before. Combined with the dark, quiet night and the freedom of being unsupervised, however, the seduction was irresistible.

Key glowing in my hand, I boldly marched to the ancient unlicensed Hudson and dared it to start. That old car couldn't resist the challenge any more than I could ignore the double dare of the brass key.

That Sunday night was typical of our small mountain valley town. The sidewalks didn't unroll from Saturday night until Monday morning. Nothing stirred. I flung my usually obedient sense of responsibility off my shoulders like the wispy scarves of fog draping the streetlights, and I triumphantly drove down the silent street.

Then the internal battle began!

"Where would your highness like to go?" I asked myself.

"Home, you idiot! You don't know what you are doing!" my conscience roared at me.

"Oh, be quiet! There is no traffic. No one is going to know. Besides, I've had three whole driving lessons!"

The objecting voice of my conscience was quiet, for a while. Using my rebellious powers of reasoning, I decided the fairground would be the most private place to exercise my driving prowess. I skirted the business district, crept passed the police station as silently as that humpbacked monster could, and started up the long, steep climb out of town. As the dirt road became steeper and steeper, that behemoth went slower and slower. Only when it chugged to a stop and started rolling backward did I remember the driving instructor saying something about downshifting. Holding in the clutch and brake, I shifted into first gear. Loose gravel and my lack of coordination prevented the car from moving forward. The rear view mirror revealed only the sharp curve at the bottom of the hill disappearing into the foggy darkness.

The dissenter within spoke again. "Okay, smarty, how are you going to get out of this one?"

A peculiar detachment enveloped me. I felt like a dispassionate bystander at a chess tournament. I coolly surveyed my options, immediately ruling out going forward, or backward. The logical choice, then, was to turn around.

The single lane road had vertical mountain walls on each side, one up and one down. On the up side, there was only more mountain face. On the down side, houses clung like barnacles to a ship. The congealed pea-soup fog prevented me from seeing into the chimney tops. I could see only the reflection of the headlights. Inching forward, the front bumper hung over fog-enshrouded rooftops. Creeping backward, the back bumper crunched mountainside. It only took 17 maneuvers to be headed in a homeward direction!

I slid that Hudson into its former parking spot as quickly as I could get my 13-year-old nerves home. The ethereal detachment had deserted me completely. I shook so hard the cold sweat dried quickly.

What a let down! There was no father, yelling at the police to do something, anything! No mother was on the front porch, wringing her hands. There was not even a little brother saying, "Boy, are you going to get it!" The house was as silent and undisturbed as I had left it. The entire town was totally unaware and uncaring of this near calamity. Even the key had lost its allure as I returned it to the desk drawer, where the secret has remained until now, over fifty years later.

Jolynne

GREAT PROGRESS

Hear, you people, condemn or praise! Computers arrived and now amaze.
Hard angular shapes, brought to your door,
angular shapes and nothing more.
Master of the world. Master or monster? Up to you to decide,
I touched the cold plastic, with its square of screen,
No heart beat, no pulse. Its bowels are out with plugs at the ends.
I made my decision, and pushed it aside.
Hark, you people, praise or curse!
Punching letters and numbers, you can write a poem or a crime prose.
No talent is required to produce a picture, computer does the job.
Who needs old masters with their oil paints and their secret mixtures!
Who needs Da Vinci, with a Mona Lisa's smile?
Old poets with beauty, music, and rhyme!
As long as a poem smells with "rotten fish,"
You'll get a prize for descriptive realism.
Computers moved the world ahead,
More millionaires sprang up from out of nowhere!
More rich, more poor. Progress is great.
Parks are full of wandering souls with deep wrinkled faces,
Sleeping nights under bridges. Awaking in the morning with shivering cold,
Tears on their faces, grey like mold.
Yuppies yakkity yakking faster than ever before, talking more, saying less,
As you see, this world makes great progress.

Tatiana

WAR

I want to shrink
And disappear,
Pretend, I am
No longer there,
In the middle of the war . . .

I am just
Ten years old
And find myself
Among the strangers
Of some sort . . .

I do not take a part
Of either side,
Just want to hide
In a disguise
Of dark rain cloud

And turn myself
Into the rain,
To weep so hard,
Until my tears
Would flood

The people hearts
And make them stop
To harm each other
In that war . . .

Lana

DESTINY

The picture is clear:
Destiny is hard to beat:
Once I tried,
But nothing ever came of it.

I pleaded and I cried
And said to her:
"This is my life,
I want to live the way

I think is best,
And not look back
Each time
I take another step."

But destiny just looked at me:
"You foolish girl,"
She said with glee:
"No matter how you try,

I always will be around
You never will be free
Not even when you thought
You did it on your own!"

Lana

AND MORE

AND MORE

BUTTRICK SAVES THE DAY

It was the end of June. Monsoon season starts soon here in Arizona.

Our friends, the Jones' moved to the northwest and we inherited their boar goat. He was more a "meat" goat than a "milking" goat and had a large belly. They called him "Rocky." However, we decided to change his name to "Buttrick" since he was always butting his head on something or someone. He was gentle most of the times, but on occasion, it was something you could not ignore because it hurt.

Our children were happy that at last we had a pet. Living out in the country, having a pet was almost compulsory. Most of their friends had cats or dogs but no one had a goat. Nine year old Danny thought it was "way cool" especially when he saw the little horns.

Seven year old Breanna thought it was nice to have a pet, but she wasn't quite sure if she liked a goat. She preferred seeing fishes swimming in a bowl. She would stare at the goat and thought of petting him, but when Buttrick lowered his head, she would quickly step back and pull her hands closer to herself. Buttrick would then throw his head back and say "ugh, ugh." This frightened Breanna and she didn't know quite what to do.

"You don't have to be scared," Danny told her. "He just wants to play."

"What if he pokes me with his horns?" she asked.

"Oh, he can't really harm anybody. He'll just butt against you," he remarked. "Just say "ugh" back to him."

"Oh, okay, if you say so," Breanna said, with an uncertain look.

Breanna began to say "ugh, ugh" everytime Buttrick came near her. Buttrick would reply with a "ugh, gugh" also and sometimes followed by a low grunt, lowering his head as he did so.

Once when Breanna turned her back after saying "ugh" to Buttrick, the goat nudged her buttocks. It startled her and caused her to lose her balance and fall on her knees to the ground. Frightened, she quickly got up and ran toward the house to me, as fast as she could. As she did, she heard Buttrick saying "gugh, gugh" as if he was laughing at her. Except for a little skinned knee, she was not really hurt. I cleaned her knee and put a band aid on.

"There, you're fine," I said, comforting her.

Thereafter, Breanna would not go close to Buttrick, but would say "gah, gugh, gah," to him from a short distance away whenever she saw him. Sometimes Buttrick would reply. Most of the times, he'd raise his head from grazing, look at her for a few seconds, then resume what he was doing. Although she wanted to pet him like Danny did, she was afraid he would butt her again. She didn't want that to happen, no, not ever again! *Someday*, she thought, *when I'm older, I'll even walk with the goat around the yard to eat grass like Danny does it and pet him too.*

One day, my husband, Richard and Danny drove into town to purchase feed for the goat and look for some chicks to raise. They also had some other errands to do.

After helping me with some household chores and reading her Sesame Street book, Breanna looked out the window and saw Buttrick near the house. She watched for a little while then decided to go outside.

"Mom," she said, "may I go outside and play?"

"Of course," I answered, "It's nice out. Just don't wander off but play close by," I added, as Breanna ran out the front door.

We lived on a ten acre property with mostly wild grass, mesquite trees, and several flowering trees and bushes. There were a number of fruit trees including peaches, pears, and plums near the house. There was a barn and another out building in the back yard, plus and enclosed area for a garden and lots of rocks around the property.

We had moved southwest from Boston, and now live near Benson where Richard got a job. We love the country as both of us grew up in a similar environment. We wanted our children to experience growing up in an area where there wasn't the hustle and bustle of a big city, nor the heavy traffic.

When Breanna saw her little bicycle near the garage, she decided to go riding, so off she went down the dirt road. After riding for a little while, she found it was no fun going down the bumpy road and hitting a rock or two every so often . . . She turned around and headed back towards the house. Just then, she heard Buttrick grunting but couldn't see him. As she got closer to the house, she noticed that the sun was no longer shining and there were some dark clouds gathering in the sky. She heard more loud grunting from Buttrick.

From a distance, she could hear some rumbling of thunder. She pedaled faster toward the house. Turning the corner, she saw Buttrick a short distance away, half hidden by some tall grass. Nearing the house, she got off her bike, and slowly walked toward the goat. Buttrick looked up briefly and said "ugh, gugh, gugh" then started munching on the grass.

"Gugh, gugh" said Breanna, as another sound of thunder was heard. This time it was louder. Breanna was closer to the goat who raised his head again. There was more rumbling and the sky lit up. Breanna wanted to get closer to Buttrick before returning to the house. As she did, the sky brightened up again as lightning struck a fairly short distance away. A loud rumbling filled the air. This frightened Breanna and caused her to jump and scream. Buttrick was also startled and jumped, raising his front legs then started to run close to Breanna toward shelter. She screamed again when she saw the goat so close as if he would run right into her. He didn't. But Breanna screamed as he passed by her. Her scream was drowned by another sudden crackling in the sky.

Buttrick did not run far but started to act wild several feet away from where Breanna was. Though still sobbing and trembling, she summoned enough courage to turn and run toward the house. Suddenly, it started to rain, then a downpour.

Concerned by the sudden change in weather, I was out the front door calling for Breanna when the lightning had struck. I heard Breanna's screaming and crying as she ran toward the back. By then, Buttrick was wild, jumping furiously up and down, kicking and grunting.

"Momma, Momma," cried Breanna, "Buttrick is mean! He scared me!" she shouted as she ran to her mother.

"Are you okay? Did he hurt you? Do you hurt anywhere?" I asked anxiously.

"No, . . . but he scared me, Momma! And the thunder scared me! she uttered. "And the lightning really scared me too!" she added sobbing. "Oh Momma, I'm so glad you came," she added, "please, Momma, don't let Buttrick get me. I'm scared of him. He's not nice."

I quickly carried my daughter to the house, turning back to look at Buttrick. By now, it was raining heavily, and she could not see the goat. Poor goat, I thought, he must be as frightened as Breanna.

About forty minutes later, as suddenly as the rain had started to pour, the downpour stopped and it was now only drizzling. Some rumblings of thunder could still be heard, but the dark blanket of clouds that rolled in overhead was gone. Breanna stopped crying but still wanted to be held.

Before long, Richard and Danny came home. We were still sitting on the couch and simply enjoying each others company as I hummed a tune holding hands. It stopped raining outside.

"Did it storm here too?" asked Danny. "It was pretty bad in town. Dad had to pull to the side of the road 'cause the windshield couldn't move fast enough for Dad to see," he said excitedly. "It was bad!"

Richard nodded his head in agreement and said, "I've never seen anything happen so fast like that before. No wonder this is called the monsoon season. I even saw a lightning bolt that struck sideways! It was awesome!" he added as he shook his head from side to side.

"Yeah, and you know what?" said Breanna as she jumped off my lap. Not waiting for a reply, she continued excitedly. "Buttrick scared me. And you know what else? Buttrick got scared of the thunder and lightning too, and was acting crazy, and I cried because I got more scared, huh, Momma, huh?"

"He sure did, didn't he? But I guess goats get scared too. Maybe we ought to go check and see how he's doing now out there," suggested Mom.

"Yeah, let's go see him. The ground is pretty wet so he must be soaked," said Dad. "Bring some towels outside, Danny," he added. "The old ones," Mom said, as we all started out the door.

Once outside, we found Buttrick pretty much where Breanna and I saw him last. He was now quiet and grazing as before the storm.

"Guess the storm caused him to act up too," I said as Danny brought out some towels.

"I'll dry him," offered Danny, approaching Buttrick. "Gugh, gaaa," he said, as he got closer to the goat. Danny suddenly stopped short near Buttrick.

"Holy Cow!" he shouted excitedly, "Mom! Dad! Breanna,! Come quick, come see this! You gotta see this!" he said, looking at the ground, waving one arm beckoning them to come. "Wow, I've never seen anything like this before! Dad look! Golly, Mom, Buttrick got it," he said pointing to the ground nearby, as his Mom, Dad, and sister quickly joined him.

"Oh, my goodness," I gasped, pulling Breanna closer to me.

"Wow! Good boy, Buttrick," said Dad happily as he petted their goat, "and thank you so much." He was overjoyed. For there on the ground, stretched out with it's head crushed, was a dead, diamond back rattler.

Breanna gasped, then scrambled down from my arms, and went to Buttrick. Frightened or not, she gave Buttrick a quick, big hug then ran back to me.

"Gugh, gugh, gugh," said Buttrick. Everyone started to laugh. They hugged and petted him. They were so grateful he was there. Breanna was no longer frightened of him, but was still a little leery about getting too close to him. They were all smiling.

Loretta

TO DO OR NOT TO DO

Panic and indecision were like a physical pain. What to do? To do nothing was going to cause death by exposure or worse, to be killed by predators. Her parents had made it very clear that to touch and leave her scent would also cause death, by the adults.

"Do I run for help? If I do, they may wander off and get lost. If I pick them up, they will die." Dancing from foot to foot, first forward, then backward, seven-year old Molly watched the inch-long pink, hairless baby bunnies crawl sightlessly over the ground. The buck and doe in the hutch seemed oblivious to their babies falling through the chicken wire of the cage.

Suddenly, with the spurting start of a competitive sprinter, Molly dashed toward the house, sobbing, "Mom, mom, they are going to die." Gasping through tears, she wailed, "You've got to do something. The babies got out and they are going to die. What can we do? We can't touch them or they'll be killed. It's too cold for them outside and they'll get lost. The dog will get them." At last she ran out of breath, giving her mother time to ask what the crisis was.

"Slow down, Molly. Now take a deep breath and tell me. What do you want me to do?"

There seemed to be no words to explain the agonizing dilemma. The only possible solution seemed to lead to certain death for the newest additions to the family menagerie. All she could think to do was tug her mother out to the rabbit hutch and point out the wriggling pink mass of infant rabbits.

Patiently, quietly, carefully, her mother lifted the newly birthed wigglers into her apron and carried them back to the nesting box in the hutch where they should have been safe. Molly continued to sob at the bleak future she expected, still aching over a hopeless helplessness she had never before experienced.

"We did the only thing we could for them. Now we just have to leave them alone. Their momma will check to see if they are all right," her mother explained. She then went back to her household chores; just as if she didn't even care that a whole family was going to die. Couldn't she see that this was a crisis of shattering magnitude?

Molly had no words for the desolation she felt. She received no comfort or reassurance that everything would be all right. She just knew it wouldn't be all right, that only doom would follow, and she was the only one who cared. She wanted to stay by the hutch, encouraging the grown rabbits to accept their returned offspring. She wanted to make them understand that it was an accident, not the babies' fault. But her mother had insisted that she leave the rabbits alone in peace to adjust. All she could do was watch, tearfully, from afar. Only total emotional and physical exhaustion took her away from her vigil on the back porch steps.

Family and school activities prevented her, much to her frustration, from checking on the rabbit family for a few days. By then she was afraid to check, not wanting to see little bunny corpses, but also afraid not to check. Inspired, she finally sent her little brother, Daniel, to look.

Daniel came back to excitedly report three tiny white fuzzies. Since he didn't seem to be traumatized, she decided there must not be any bodies lying around, and it would be safe to look for herself.

Houdini, Evel Knievel and Merlina grew up to have families of their own. The *great escape* was never repeated, and Molly never asked herself what became of the rest of the rescued litter. It was just too horrible to contemplate.

JoLynne

WINTER
IN SIERRA VISTA, AZ

I couldn't believe my eyes
When I looked outside,
Winter Wonderland,
That's what I saw
And everything
Was covered with snow . . .
The pine tree
In front of my house,
The roof, the fence,
The rest of the plants
Were all capped
With the snow!

And if that, wasn't
Enough for the show,
Dark sky was still letting go
More and more
Of the whirling snow,
With snowflakes
Dancing in the air,
Never falling straight
Upon the earth,
But curling, and floating,
Teasing and flirting,
Finally landing
Where no one expected.

Lana

WANDERING . . .

I wonder what New Year
Will bring,—more wars,
Or even worse,
The Aliens would land
On planet Earth?

Or else,—the tallest ocean wave
That we have ever seen
Would sweep away
The people and the land?

One may never know, unless,
We peek into the box
Where all Tomorrows are stacked
And hidden far away from us . . .

Some people claimed,
They found the box one day,
But as they tried to reach for it
It disappeared, right in front of their eyes . . .

Lana

I SAW ALL THIS

I saw a silvery bird trembling and caught by searchlights
    on the black, velvety sky.
I watched them shoot this bird—shattered to dust,
    and absorbed by the night.

I heard the sounds of victory on one side of the front.
    And tearing cries on the opposite side.
I sensed the tears and sorrows of the ones who were left
    alone—without a husband, or son, or loved one.
I saw all this and much more.

I witnessed a pilot parachuting down—wounded, still alive—
    but the burst of lit bullets of yellow, orange, and red,
Shot . . . the lifeless body sprawled
    on the naked, hard branches of a tree. Left there.

While snow flakes were softly falling,
    covering white blanket,
Covering the SHAME of EVIL WAR.
    I saw all this and much more.

Tatiana

MY JOURNAL

My journal will never famous be,
Nor interesting to anyone but me.
But I'll try to keep an account of my life,
That my family and posterity may someday read.

But I've not been very diligent you see,
In writing in my journal faithfully,
This responsibility was not a priority,
As activities for family, work, and others seem to be.

Tomorrow, I said, tomorrow I'll sit and write
The happenings of today
Often times tomorrow came and went
And before I ever wrote anything, time passed away.

And now I reflect and look upon
My journal that sometimes I've written in,
And I wonder what took place, how did I feel?
What did I do? Can I fill the empty spaces within?

I hope and pray I'll have the time
To make amends and start to be more diligent
And be more faithful as I grow older
To be more careful and consistent.

For the Lord will surely ask someday of me,
"Open up your journal, my child, and share it with me."
Will I be ready and glad to show?
What I have done while on earth below?

Loretta

THE UNKNOWN

What is this mystery called death?
I asked in a pensive mood.

The aged and weary say it is rest
After life's long work is through.

The troubled in spirit call it peace,
Release from the world's cares.

The broken hearted think it comfort
Escape from all despair.

And the faithless call it nothing,
A blackness without end.

I would call it a beacon
On a pathway to a Friend.

Mary
Written at age 16

THERE WERE FOUR

They were four—four little girls.
They were so different and yet the same.
From different countries, different religions
and yet they were the same.
They were young, with hopes for life,
with hopes for love, for they were young!
But an Evil War came in their way
It took away the precious dreams and loved ones.
The Evil War, the Evil War.

Tatiana

IT SAYS HERE . . . .

Some people put great stock in their horoscopes as a way to anticipate their future. I've found that Chinese fortune cookies have more accuracy for me. However, the outcome is never quite what I have expected. For instance, a fortune cookie prediction of "Expect endless affection from tall, dark and handsome," led me to believe that an Antonio Banderas look-alike would have eyes only for me. Reality? When I opened my front door, a huge black dog knocked me down and thoroughly washed my face!

Now, most people receive generic fortune cookie messages about having success in business, receiving money from a distant relative, or having an interesting love life. Can't you just imagine an impersonal machine stamping out those fortunes, with a bored assembly-line worker packaging them by choosing three dozen from Column A and four dozen from Column B? I believe that somewhere there is an ancient Chinese monk inscrutably meditating on special fortunes to tantalize and torment me. I'm still puzzling over the one that read, "You will have a potential urge."

I go for months at a time avoiding fortune cookies, but then have a craving to have just one more. It's a sickness with me. I try to resist and then, *wham*, The Ancient One has blind-sided me again. One day, I gave in to temptation and had lunch at the Golden Dragon. My fortune cookie read, "Humor and color will sweeten your life."

Now, who could resist such a harmless and pleasant message? On my way back to work, I picked up a cake from the bakery for a co-worker's birthday. As I was crossing the parking lot, the cake and I were run down by a clown on a bicycle carrying a bouquet of balloons!

You know, on second thought I am going to give up on fortune cookies and start reading my horoscope. The last fortune cookie I had said: "You should presently begin to play with a full deck."

JoLynne

218

CAN YOU BEAT THAT?

After fifteen years, they let me go.
Now, I'm on unemployment row.
Struggled hard and worked at length,
So what do I get for my talents and strength?
A letter of thanks, "You've been just great,
But sorry, we can't use you now, so there's the gate."
Can you beat that? Can you beat that?

They don't even ask, how do I feel? How do I feel?
What can you expect? What can I feel?
Well, I feel rotten, rotten and betrayed.
And to be honest, I am quite dismayed!
I don't know where to go, I don't know where to turn.
But do you think they care? They're not being burned.
Can you beat that? Can you beat that?

There was a guy the other day,
Looking for a job with decent pay.
Been in school most of his life
Got his Master's and a brand new wife.
Has plenty of bills, but not many practical skills.
Was waved good bye, 'cause he was overqualified
Can you beat that? Can you beat that?

Before I left, another fellow came in,
Wanting a job and got his application in.
The boss saw him standing, smiled and says "hello"
Then talked about a party and an after dinner show.
I heard it wasn't long after I left the place,
The other fellow sat at the desk and took my space.
Can you beat that? Can you beat that?

Loretta

LIFE

As I walk along the path of life
I try not to dwell on my chances lost,
There's no way I can bring them back
And start all over, like a cigarette pack!

There were some joys, but sorrows too,
Misery, hunger and World War Two,
We lived through hell, but survived,
Thanking Heavens for saving our lives . . .

And, to make a long story—short,
We landed on the opposite side of the globe,
In the beautiful city of Angels,
Where there was—not a hint of a smog!

Lana

THE ROLE OF MOTHERHOOD

We must remember the role of motherhood
For motherhood is sacred, motherhood is holy.
The role of motherhood is on all women,
Endowed by noble rights and created by divinity.

A call for all women, bearing a child or not,
In all walks of life, for all eternity.
For it is the essence of who we are as women.
It is a gift, a privilege to be protected, in all humility.

Are we living our lives to be up to that challenge?
Are we living our lives to be true?
Are we nurturing, loving, and teaching the children?
Are we building faith and strength in God too?

Remember our first mother, Eve?
Whose strength, faith, and courage endured,
Led the way for the role of motherhood to be,
Led the way for mothering to be.

Yes, let us remember our first mother, Eve,
Who set the example for all women on earth.
The mother of all living who brought us our birth,
Bound by covenant, ensured God's plan here on earth.

Loretta

THROUGH THE SPIRIT OF LOVE

The music of the Sabbath morn
Touched so my longing heart,
"I am a Child of God," I heard,
Oh, what a beautiful message to impart.

I feel the love of God surround me,
As the words of the song unfold.
He sent me here on earth to live,
To learn, to grow, to hearken parables retold.

He'll lead me and He'll guide me,
If I have Him by my side.
And I'll find my way back to Him
If I but learn to live His laws and abide.

The song is sung with familiar words,
Then sung in other tongues.
And the Spirit of love still permeates
The message of Heavenly Father's throng.

"I Am a Child of God" I know,
By the Spirit of love that tells me so.
In English or Micronesiam, Indian or French,
The message is clear for me to enhance.

Loretta

FILLING SPACES

Empty places, dark and weary,
Echoing, aching, empty places
Placenta of self-pity
Nourishing bitterness and discontent.

Discouragement aborted
By gentle challenge,
The way, preparing,
Urging on growth, new life.

Spaces fill, spilling
To overflow,
Perhaps to fill
Your empty places.

JoLynne

AUTUMN

The autumn came
So silently and quiet
I hardly noticed it
Until I went outside.

And there it was,
Unmistakably clear,
The falling leaves
And cooling
Autumn breeze.

Hot summer days,
I thought, would never end
And constant scene
Of bright blue skies
Would never change!

But here they are,
The dark-gray skies
With heavy clouds
And blazing sun
Nowhere in sight!

Lana

WINTER

Winter finally is here
After a very long fall

And the mountain peaks
Are covered with snow.

The air is crisp,
The sun is bright

And birds are singing
With all their might,

But very soon
It all will end

And the summer heat
Will be here again.

Lana

WHAT IS THIS THING CALLED DEATH?

A friend just died recently after a long and painful illness,
Though sad that she is gone, I felt peace and comfort
Knowing she was now free from physical pain and suffering.

But how did I feel when my sister lost her newborn at childbirth
Having lived but a few short hours with abnormal breathing.
I was bereaved. But, she, devastated at her loss, crying.

A young man, a recent high school graduate, served his country.
Less than a year later, his mom called, told me he was coming home
In a casket, she said, fighting back tears, her voice cracking.

A young mother of two children, a daughter of a long time friend,
Saved her children, but was engulfed by smoke, a burning home
Never again, to see her family here—playing, working, loving.

A friendly neighbor nearby hid his feelings from others
Apparently became so depressed, ending his life here on earth
Leaving family, friends, and more wondering, sad, and grieving.

Then my grandmother, in the twilight of her life
Asks God to take her for she's lived a long life and is tired.
Next day, she's not at lunch but found in bed-lifeless but smiling.

So what is this thing we call death, for we all must pass its portal
Is it the end of everything we know to be meaningful?
Or is it in fact life beyond this earth with death as its beginning?

As Holy Scriptures does reveal, a life before birth on earth
So wouldn't life here on earth, be a part of our eternal venture?
And life hereafter, according to how we lived on earth,
the eternal plan of God, our Creator?

Loretta

HUMBLE CONTRIBUTION

(Ode to Myself)

A humble contribution to the big world—
My name was written three thousand times
Or a little more,
Placed on walls of many people's homes,
Written with big letters under painted
Landscapes, florals, and more . . .
Each picture painted with LOVE and part of my SOUL.
Therefore I left my humble mark on the world,
Three thousand times,
Or a little more.

Tatiana

WE ARE HIS HANDS

We are His hands.
And as His children, we can express His love
By providing comfort and a listening ear
Sharing our blessings and His love from above.

We are His hands
As we display compassion for each other,
Developing friendships, rendering service when needed,
Extending our talents and skills with one another.

We are His hands
As we come to know burdens, hardships of one another
The sadness, frustrations, and challenges too,
But also, share joys, successes, and peace we encounter.

We are His hands,
With faith, courage, trust, we are strengthened by His power
Growing as His children through His teachings,
For He created our being, God, our Heavenly Father.

Loretta

ALL IN A WEEK'S WORK

MONDAY'S child is fair of face.

TUESDAY'S child is full of grace

WEDNESDAY'S child is full of woe.

THURSDAY'S child has far to go.

FRIDAY'S child is loving and giving,

SATURDAY'S child works hard for a living.

And the child born on the SABBATH DAY is fair and wise and good
and gay . . .

MONDAY: Laundry

Basements, dark and damp. Steamy, chlorine bleach laden air. Hot,
heavy, wet clothes mom-handled up narrow stairs to sunshine, building
vapor clouds in crisp morning air. Peg clothespins with teeth marks in the
top. Sun-warmed, wind-whipped, air-freshened clean clothes dried to a
rough stiffness. Huge piles of whites, darks, work clothes, towels and sheets.
The free-associated images of laundry days in a long-ago childhood.

Washday also meant wearing the poorest clothes in our wardrobe while
our more presentable ones were made wearable again.

Visions of the fearsome wringer, with memories of being ordered to hit the release bar to free a hand, sometimes up to mid-arm, from the toothless jaws.

Weary irritability was the regular seasoning of the supper, which had simmered on the back of the stove all day.

Folding the towels and sheets with their special enveloping fragrance was the reward for enduring yet another washday.

TUESDAY: Ironing

Work clothes in the bottom, dark clothes, light and then white shirts—clothes again sorted, sprinkled, rolled and refrigerated in their special zippered plastic bag. Hiss and steam as hot iron touched damp cottons, releasing another distinct fragrance. Standing on tiptoe, scavenging clothes hangers from the closets. Rows of starched white shirts and properly creased trousers hanging from doorframes, leaving only a child-sized tunnel through the doorway.

Radio music—Benny Goodman, the Dorsey brothers and of course, Glen Miller, accompanied by the scent of starch weaving through the flimsy wire tangle of pants creasers.

WEDNESDAY: Mending

White lines on print dresses where the hem had been let down. Ingeniously placed knee patches on pants in an attempt to avoid looking like patches. Replacing lost buttons was a first sewing lesson. The fascination of sock mending on a burned-out lightbulb. How could these tiny stitches weave back and forth through the sock without hurting the lightbulb? And did you know that Sue's mom had a wooden thing called a "darning egg" she used for sock mending?

THURSDAY: Baking

Wonderful aromas escaping the house to beckon across the front porch. Baking day was not restricted to desserts and breads in the oven. There was always something stewing, slow-simmering on the back burner of the stove, perhaps a chicken waiting the addition of homemade noodles, rolled thin, sliced and spread on newspaper on the kitchen table to dry. Childish pride came from a successful assault on the still gummy noodles.

Stacks of cooling cookies enticed a conspiracy of using a staged diversion as cover for a grab-and-run, leading to the inevitable argument over who "earned" the majority of the spoils. An even split was no fun without the spice of the argument first.

If company was coming, something special would be in the making, maybe a pie of homemade mincemeat made with real meat, suet, apples, raisins and spices. Thursday was always a very good day!

FRIDAY: Cleaning

The roar of the vacuum cleaner. The shaking of rugs. The removal of miniscule dust-bunnies from the fluffy floor mop. Dustcloths, furniture polish and the window-polishing equipment of newspapers and vinegar. Injunctions to work from the top down. Licks and promises. And thumps on the back of the head!

Spring and fall housecleaning from bottom to top. Curtains hung on clotheslines to air, rugs to be beaten to free trapped dust. Closets emptied and organized. Childhood "treasures" added to the trash pile.

SATURDAY: Shopping

Farmers' pickups parked on main street from early in the morning, news of commodity and hog prices exchanged over coffee at the counter of the only café in town. Men in overalls hanging out at the Ford garage or the hardware store while wives paid duty calls to the drugstore, grocery store and five-and-dime. Kids and dogs chasing each other noisily in whatever direction avoided attention of parents.

Gossip in the produce aisle, in front of the meat counter, in the checkout line, and eventually at the soda fountain in the drug store.

Visiting friends or relatives for supper and more gossip, often accompanied by endless games of Canasta or Pinochle. Kids playing tag in the street under the street lights, or inventing their own team chase game of "Follow the Arrow," ending in the inevitable nap on the backseat of the car or in the pickup bed on the way home.

SUNDAY: Church

Kids walking to Sunday School in their best, with injunctions of "Don't get dirty!" ringing in their ears. Grandmas and other older people slowly making their way into the sanctuary of the church, Methodist, Lutheran or Catholic alike. Church bells ringing at each end of town, in competition for the most parishioners.

Hurry home to change clothes before the predictable scramble for the Sunday comics while dinner was in final preparation.

Hoping for the chicken wishbone, just once for a change, and that there wouldn't be canned peas again. Forcing room for dessert, whatever it was, to go down on an overload of mashed potatoes and gravy

Watching the elders (men, that is) take a brief snooze while the table was cleared and the dishes washed (by the women). A final look at the funnies while ZZZZZ drift in the air. Waiting for the best of all, a Sunday drive to unknown and often uncharted destinations, with another opportunity to nap in the backseat of the car on the darkened trip home. If you are lucky, you get carried to bed without even waking up!.

JoLynne

FAITH IN LIVING

That Christmas comes but just once a year
Our calendar makes abundantly clear,
But what would happen to me and to you
If we lived it each day as He taught us to do?

People of faith know the Spirit of love,
Of power and sound mind from the Father above.
Oh, why do we live in fear, war and hate,
And not care for each other before it's too late?

Oh, Father, you give us our daily bread
And thru the valley we're safely led.
In arms that span from crib to the cross
There's no room for sin or for the dross.

So let our praises and hosannas ring
As we live the words in carols we sing
Of love, joy and peace, and ever good will,
And serving each other, because He loves us still.

JoLynne

HAIKU

LITTLE LAMB

With short, brownish fur,
And eyes barely open,
A little lamb is born.

RED ROSE

Soft, velvety petals,
Blossoming in the light,
A lovely red rose.

WHITE BUNNY

Hopping across a field,
Stopping to look around,
A cute, white bunny.

A GARDENIA

With soft, white petals
And beautiful fragrance,
A lovely gardenia.

VOLCANIC FUMES

Gargantuan mass
Against a brilliant sky,
The volcanic fumes.

*   *   *

A LIMERICK

There was a little fellow named Last,
Whose family was always having a blast,
The youngest of thirteen,
He often was seen,
Hiding like a snake in the grass.

Loretta

THANKSGIVING

Thanksgiving Day is coming,
The most important holiday
And I didn't mean
Pre-Christmas sale!

But—the gathering of family
At least once a year,
On that important day
To be together like before,

And give our thanks to God
For all the blessings
That we hold
From the Heaven above.

To reminisce and make few jokes
On brother, sister, or them both,
To laugh, and cry for someone,
Who isn't with us anymore . . .

But hope and pray that he or she
Is now in a better world!

Lana